T0328504

RUSSIAN ACADEMY OF SCIENCES

INSTITUTE FOR AFRICAN STUDIES

AFRICAN STUDIES IN RUSSIA

Works of the Institute for African Studies of the Russian Academy of Sciences

Yearbook 2014–2016

MOSCOW

Institute for African Studies RAS

2017

This Edition:
© MEABOOKS Inc.
ISBN: 978-1-988391-06-9 (print)
ISBN: 978-1-988391-07-6 (eBook)

MEABOOKS Inc.
34 CH. DU BOISE
LAC-BEAUPORT
QC G3B 2A5
CANADA
www.meabooks.com

ISBN 978-5-91298-202-6
© Institute for African Studies RAS, 2017
© Authors, 2017
© Abisheva G.M., design, 2017

CONTENTS

Articles

Synopsis

ARTICLES

Irina Abramova

POTENTIAL OF THE AFRICAN CONTINENT IN THE UPDATED STRATEGY OF DEVELOPMENT OF THE RUSSIAN FEDERATION

At present, the horizons for the development of the Russian economy are largely constrained by the narrowing potential and gradual exhaustion of the current model of economic development, still largely based on the exports of raw materials and other primary products. The mistaken choice by post-Soviet reformers of an unlimited reliance on future foreign investment and the good will of the global market brought about broad-scale deindustrialisation and a historically unprecedented outflow of national wealth and capital, aggravated by ever increasing external political and military pressure and Western economic sanctions.

According to expert estimates, the combined costs of financial sanctions and the fall in oil prices cost Russia about 0.6 trillion dollars over 2014–2017 period. In these conditions the goals of development strategy outlined by the President of Russia underscore the necessity of an immediate real restructuring of the economy on the basis of its innovative modernisation and diversification. A significant role in the formation of such a mechanism can be played by the intensification of economic activity in the markets of those countries which today are more open and inclined to cooperate with Russia, on the one hand, and have significant resource and growth prospects, on the other. In my opinion African countries belong to such category.

So far, the current Russian strategies of economic development have been employing the opportunities provided by African markets for the purposes of the recovery and diversification of domestic manufacturing, the construction industry, the infrastructure, and the services sector to rather a small extent. Meanwhile, the African track opens a window of opportunity to restore and boost industries, other than those of the primary sector, in Russia, as well as to sharpen skills and upgrade mechanisms of penetration into highly competitive developed and transition economies. This is exactly what China did in the 1980s and 1990s when it was only about to become a global economic power.

Over the recent years the leading world powers and the centres of economic power came to realise that the resources and human and economic potential of Africa are of high value for the world economy and the new model of global development now in formation. It follows that all the countries which claim to be global actors in the international arena and future world economy are expanding into the African market, rich in resources and mineral reserves. Their objective is to secure their global positions by investing into the emerging economic chains. Such an approach allows to go beyond trade relations with African countries, and to gain a foothold in Africa for the future, guaranteeing an inflow of a substantial amount of the continent's exclusive resources for their own, including innovative, development in the new economic environment.

Today the old and new actors of the world economy have engaged into tough geo-economic and geo-political scramble for Africa. The apples of discord are natural resources, growing markets, human resources, and the sympathy of the most rapidly growing continent. Political gains also matter as they add to economic co-operation with Africa. African states make up almost a quarter of the voting members at the UN and other organisations. Their support is an important strategic reserve in the global diplomatic arena, vital for the establishment of a joint force in the process of restructuring existing institutions, mechanisms, and structures of global governance, and altering the balance of power in the world.

The economic weight of Africa is on the rise. Over the last few years, major think tanks, consulting and rating agencies, investment banks and research centres from many countries have repeatedly stated that the 21st century will see Africa as the most rapidly developing region – a region that will define the pattern and the growth rate of developed countries. This will also have a bearing on the issues of raw materials, energy resources, and human capital. The penetration into African markets and the synergy between the Old World and Africa are necessary goals for Europe if it is to retain its geopolitical weight and maintain living standards on the same level as in the 21st century. For China, Russia, and other BRICS countries, as well as the United States (US), both resources and geopolitics rank high on the national agenda, which makes it essential to co-operate with Africa.

In recent years, Africa has no longer been considered a backward region on the periphery of the world. Globalisation accounted for a rapid growth of size, diversity, inter-connectedness, and inter-dependence at the levels of state and of interpersonal relations alike. This resulted in a shift in the world economy, with countries swapping their roles and inequality being fossilised as a new global economic model takes shape.

Brought by globalisation, the current trends in the world economy put African countries on the back foot. With the changes in the late 20th century, the role of Africa saw no changes for the better. To make matters worse, the African share in the international markets shrank even further and the continent stood little chance of 'plugging in' the world economy on an equal footing. As developed countries transitioned to a post-industrial and innovative development model, Africa's economy fell further behind. True, as for macroeconomic indicators and HDI, most African countries are still lagging behind (in the early 21st century the share of the continent constituted just under 2% of the global GDP, the figures for trade and investments being 3% and 5% respectively).

However, during the first decade of the 21st century, despite a global financial and economic crisis, Africa's role in the world economy started to change. [Continue the paragraph.]Over the period from 2001 to 2004, Africa's economy grew at one of the highest rates in the world. Even the considerable global economic slowdown in 2007–2010 had only minor negative impact on GDP growth in most African countries.

In terms of GDP growth, over the last 15 years Sub-Saharan Africa (SSA) has been second only to East Asia. From 2001 to 2014, 9 Sub-Saharan economies grew by at least 7% annually. In 2013, Sub-Saharan GDP grew by 5.2%. In 2014 it increased by 4.7%, the slight slowdown due a fall in fossil fuel prices. Meanwhile, the Sub-Saharan growth rate was far above the average for the world (3.5%) or the developing countries (4.3%).

The year 2015–2016 saw a less optimistic macroeconomic performance on the African continent, which could be explained by the global slowdown, a further fall in prices for raw material and fossil fuel, and a decline in demand for African products, combined with a slew of political crises and a rise of terrorist threat.

The average growth rate in SSA fell to 3.1% in terms of nominal prices and to 3.3% in terms of purchasing power parity (PPP) in 2015, with the corresponding figures (estimates) in 2016 being 1.5% and 1.7% respectively. A number of SSA countries, namely Ethiopia, Ivory Coast, Tanzania, and Rwanda, managed to retain a rather high, if lower than before, growth rate of 7–9%.

Over the past two decades, the countries of SSA have formed an economic area that in terms of its pace of development and growing political and economic influence is approaching that of "emerging" countries with developing market economies, notably the BRICS countries. An array of Western think tanks (MSCI, Economist Intelligence Unit, McKinsey and Ernst and Young) hold that the investment climate in Africa is gradually getting more attractive compared to the Chinese and Indian ones. The forecast of the

World Bank predicts that "just like China 30 years ago and India 20 years ago, the African continent is about to "take off". The perception of Africa as a poverty-stricken and backward continent with dire prospects does not correspond to reality any longer. True, a lot is yet to be done. Yet step by step SSA is catching up.

The rating agency Standard and Poor's lists markets with the most favourable investment climate. The section Frontier Emerging Markets (37 countries in total) includes 8 SSA countries, namely Botswana, Ivory Coast, Ghana, Kenya, Mauritius, Namibia, Nigeria, and Zimbabwe.

Some experts expect the average GDP growth rate in SSA to level off at 5–7% in the coming decade (from 2020 onwards). Western think tanks (EY, RAND, FUTURES, just to name a few) forecast that if the current economic and demographic macro-trends remain in place by 2050, the African economy will stand every chance of soaring from $2 trillion to $29 trillion to overtake the US and Europe combined.

The estimates (Rand, Stanford University, Shanghai Military University and Research Institute) are that from 2030 onwards Africa (as a whole) will turn into the *global strategic reserve of raw materials second to none*. First and foremost, the issue on the table is reserves of strategic and military relevance, indispensable for the military and strategic development in the 21st century. If we consider non-ferrous and rare metals, indispensable in, say, the production of engines for long-range bombers, we find that the US military industrial complex imports over 50% of rare metals from SSA (DRC, Zimbabwe). In fact, the figure for cobalt is 75 per cent.

Another reason why the relevance of the African economy is on the rise is that *the African population is growing rapidly and its demographic composition is undergoing drastic changes*. In 2009, the population of Africa exceeded 1 billion and its growth rate is the highest on the planet. By 2020, the African labour force will surpass 700 million, and by 2050,1.5 billion. We have to understand that, in several decades, Africa will define the demographic and social world map.

These are general estimates of Western researchers, clarifying why the leading economic hubs have engaged in a "Scramble for Africa" in the early 21st century. [Continue the paragraph.]

All the countries which follow the trend and have already been yielding or are just at the point of starting to yield "the African dividend" (as they benefit from their co-operation with countries of the African continent) will manage to avoid marginalisation in the world economy. Let us give more thought to the words of one of the former Chinese leaders, who said that 15%

of China's economic success comes from the efficient co-operation with Africa.

Africa has embarked on the task of attracting foreign investors, ensuring a more favourable investment climate. The estimates are that in the decade to come foreign investment-oriented policy will add about 2% to the African GDP. Western countries, which had been the first to gain a foothold in the region, changed the discourse on co-operation with Africa. The focus was shifted from "development aid" to "partnership", i.e. joint exploitation of resources to tap into the potential of the continent on a mutually beneficial basis. New actors go neck to neck with the Western economic centres.

Africa is highly attractive for foreign investors since the return on investment in Africa is tangibly higher than that in other developing areas.

In 2015, the African share in the global foreign direct investment (FDI) accounted for 8%, with the number of investment projects implemented on the African soil reaching 705 (4% from all the investment projects in the world).

The 2010s are showing a trend towards a higher share of SSA in the total FDI, with Nigeria, South Africa, Mozambique, Ivory Coast, Senegal, Cameroon, Kenya, Ghana, Uganda, and Tanzania contributing the most.

Transnational companies from developing countries build up their activities in Africa, with developed countries still ruling the roost. In terms of total investment, in 2015 the first place went to Italy, which was followed by the US and Great Britain. With its FDI relatively small, China, however, stands out for creating new jobs for Africa. Thus, 32 investment projects implemented by China in 2015 created 14,127 jobs.

When it comes to how investments are distributed between industries, new trends take shape, i.e. the share of fossil fuel is in decline and the share of manufacturing and service is on the rise, with the services sector accounting for over 75% of the total FDI. A graphic example here is investments in energy, mostly renewable, which in 2015 matched those in mining in absolute value and in percentage alike.

As far as the structure of FDI is concerned, the biggest part is made up by manufacturing, IT, and education – the branches vital for economic modernisation and catching up with the emerging model of the world development.

However, the mining industry is still there to attract FDI, since it takes time to diversify investments and switch to cutting-edge industries. Urbanisation coupled with the emerging middle class brings to the table wholesale and retail trade. Presently, over 150 projects are being implemented in the sectors of IT, telecommunications, trade, and consumer goods, and a further 120 – in the financial sector. All in all, these account for a hefty 50% of all the projects funded by FDI.

China is a role model for other governments to promote national companies across Africa. Unlike European states, which are focused on financial and credit services and ODA, China places emphasis on trade and investment.

A rising economic power undergoing a trade and investment boom, China has become a competitive alternative to Western countries. At the second international conference on the development of African markets convened by UNDP in Abidjan on 28–30 March 2017, most African leaders, ministers and businessmen mentioned the immense Chinese contribution to the socio-economic development of Africa.

China's active and highly beneficial co-operation with Africa pushed other developing countries to build up their activities on the continent. In particular, these include India, with a trade turnover with Africa of over $60 billion, and Turkey and Brazil with $20 billion and $17 billion respectively.

In general, our foreign partners have set up effective state institutes and foundations designed to support national business on African soil. Until recent times, France had the Ministry of Co-operation with former colonies. The US set up the United States Agency for International Development (USAID), with a range of programmes hammered out and put into practice – a case in point is a programme on improving trade relations with SSA (African Growth and Opportunity Act – AGOA). China, India, and Turkey developed state institutions and financial agencies aimed at developing and encouraging co-operation with African states. This is how public-private partnership serves the national interest.

These days African states are shaping new approach in their relations with the rest of the world, pursuing more beneficial international economic co-operation. African leaders have come to realizes that, given the current population of the continent and the population growth, there is an opportunity to transform Africa into an influential economic union and an immensely big common market, but for that they need to develop a synergistic approach.

It is high time that Russia followed suit with a clear understanding of how it can benefit from this co-operation in geo-political and geo-economic terms, how such co-operation may help Russia to achieve its objectives, i.e. to strengthen its position in the international arena, to boost its economy, and to raise the living standards of Russian citizens.

It is feasible to achieve all these goals provided that we arrange political and economic co-operation with the African continent in a wise and sensible manner. We should design a sensible state policy and keep our fingers on the pulse. A *conditio sine qua non* here is that experts monitor the process on a regular basis and that we do not seek a quick return.

Russia is further building up co-operation with African partners on a wide range of global and regional issues, namely ensuring international stability, strengthening the role of the UN, fighting international terrorism and seeking ways to prevent regional conflicts. What testifies to Russia's urge to develop relations with African countries is that in 2014 the Russian Ministry of Foreign Affairs set up a post of Special Envoy for relations with African regional organisations.

Russia supports the Africans in their desire to tackle domestic challenges (related to security and economic development) on their own and to actively engage in the shaping of the new global architecture. Clearly, social and economic progress on the continent correlates with long-lasting peace and stability. It is a pity that a number of terrorist organizations are building up their activities with the intention of destabilising the situation in many states across the African continent. Among the most dangerous ones are the Islamic State (IS, ISIS), Boko Haram, Al-Shabaab, Al-Qaeda in the Islamic Maghreb and Al-Mourabitoun, just to name a few (all banned in Russia). In this regard, we should remember that Russia supports the efforts of the Africans to lay the foundations of collective security and regional peacekeeping potential.

A premium is put on the diversification of relations with integration structures. A good example here is the African Union (AU), which has granted Russia observer status in 2006. Both Russia and the AU are deeply interested in further co-operation in line with the Memorandum of Understanding (MoU) signed in September 2014 between the Russian Ministry of Foreign Affairs and the Commission of the African Union regarding the procedure of political consultations.

Conflict and crisis resolution is high on the agenda. However, despite the aforementioned MoU and active political dialogue, our trade and economic co-operation leaves much to be desired. The same holds true for political co-operation in science and education, humanities and culture, in spite of regular consultations with the African Union on how to involve Russian companies in large-scale projects, in particular within the New Partnership for Africa's Development (NEPAD). Co-operation in education is a good example. Within the framework of humanitarian co-operation, 10 thousand African students are currently studying at Russian colleges. The exchange is to be multi-lateral since the AU has set up the Pan-African University, which unites leading African universities. This is an asset for future co-operation with prominent Russian universities. On top of that, Russia and the AU have set up a public-private partnership, with Russia donating $60m toward the fight against Ebola, development of a corresponding vaccine, construction of hospitals, administration of medical aid, and carrying out quarantines.

Active effort is taken to strengthen relations with the Southern African Development Community (SADC). Different options on improving political, trade, economic and humanitarian co-operation are being considered. Accordingly, for instance, in 2003, Russia and SADC signed a MoU on co-operation.

It is crucial that the co-operation between the Eurasian Economic Union, the African Union, and SADC is well under way, which is partly due to the joint participation of Russia and South Africa in BRICS programmes and structures.

Apart from already existing institutionalized relations between the African Union and SADC, new opportunities emerge to co-operate with regional and sub-regional structures and institutions. Russia (the USSR until 1992) as a founding member of the UN has been always actively co-operating with the UN Economic Commission for Africa (UNECA). For instance, it sent its experts and specialists to work at UNECA. Russia welcomed the adoption of the Lagos Action Plan, which pursued the establishment of the pan-African common market. The co-operation with the regional integrational group Common Market for Eastern and Southern Africa (COMESA) is coming into force, with the Economic Community of West African States (ECOWAS) and the Economic Community of Central African States (ECCAS) soon to follow.

Russia has signed a range of agreements with the League of Arab States, a pan-Arab organization which encompasses a wide range of issues for co-operation, i.e. politics, economy, social sphere. The agreement stipulates regular consultations on political issues, including the Middle East Conflict, a dialogue between civilisations, economic and humanitarian co-operation and the fight against terrorism, just to name a few.

Under the current integration processes, a plethora of inter-African co-operation institutes came to exist. For Russia, it would be most beneficial to join the African Development Bank. The estimates are that Russia would have to pay the initial membership fee of about $300m paid in three instalments over the period of 3 years. This move would provide Russia with access to the African Development Bank's loans.

We believe that co-operation with regional and sub-regional groups may benefit Russia in many ways. First and foremost, this holds true for economic co-operation.

Regretfully, we have to acknowledge that Russia is currently lacking in a full-fledged coherent foreign economic policy towards African countries. Russia's presence in this land of opportunity is mostly limited to the growing co-operation with South Africa within the BRICS format, as well as to the activities of major Russian companies, which seldom have a vision of business development in Africa. In those cases where they do have a strategy, this strategy is not really a part of any concrete national action plan for the African continent.

So far Russian-African trade co-operation leaves much be desired, with the total trade turnover hovering at about $10–12bn per year (in 2015, the figure amounted to $11.1bn, or 2.2% of the Russian foreign trade).

Noticeably, North Africa is the main Russian partner (with trade turnover at the level of $7.7bn, or 1.5% of the Russian foreign trade), while Russian exports to the Sub-Saharan Africa amounted to $2.1bn in 2015, or 0.6% of the Russian foreign trade. This figure lies within the margin of error.

Overall, our co-operation is of one-sided character, with oil products, chemical fertilizers, pulp-and-paper products, and wheat constituting a hefty 70%. In certain years, sale of military equipment came to the fore. The prospects for the Russian exports in the military and other segments are traditionally constrained by a low level of economic development in Africa, long distance between our markets, and China's edge over many traditional Russian exports.

The Russian business in Africa affects both the public and the private sector. With economic co-operation encompassing more and more areas, Africa accounts for around 1.5% of all Russia's FDI over the last 12 years (2003–2015), or $15bn. Between 60% and 70% of the investments are allocated to exploration and production of oil, gas, uranium, bauxites, and iron ore, just to name a few. Some 30 Russian companies have become engaged in this field.

Having lost a number of mineral deposits after the collapse of the Soviet Union, Russia experiences relative or absolute deficit of some mineral resources. A case in point here is manganese, chrome, bauxite, zinc, tin and some other minerals, including strategic ones.

Many Russian deposits are depleted and no longer profitable, while others are struggling to break even. It will take lots of money to develop fields beyond the Urals and in the Arctic, as new technologies and infrastructure are required. Russia desperately needs manganese (100%), chrome (80%), and cobalt, just to name a few. Production costs in Africa are usually much lower than in Russia. Russia and Africa complement each other in some mineral reserves. The bauxites imported from Africa account for over 60% of the Russian aluminium production.

Another argument for further co-operation in this sphere is Russia's solid position in the global market of raw materials. Africa's share of oil reserves and oil production makes up 14% and 12% respectively. Over the past decade, African countries have discovered new oil and gas reserves. Our relations in the energy sector are a blend of co-operation and competition. Hopefully, the former will prevail.

Not least, there is another major reason why Russia has to build up its presence on the African continent. In the long term, Russia-Africa co-operation may contribute to the diversification of the Russian economy and the improvement of the structure of Russian exports by granting access to sustainable and reliable markets. The energy sector has the highest potential (nuclear and hydro power come first), followed by mechanical engineering, chemical industry, including fertilizers, pharmacy, cutting-edge IT and co-operation in space. The African military sector is also growing rapidly. Around 11% of the heavy weaponry exported by Russia is sold to Africa. The Russian exports of heavy weaponry to Sub-Saharan Africa and North Africa account for 27% and 30% of their military imports respectively.

Russia should base its co-operation with Africa on the pursuit of clear-cut national objectives, while tackling various challenges in the way of this partnership. We have to consider not only what we can offer right now but also what we could offer in the future. What is certain is that it is high time for us to develop new forms of economic co-operation, including marketing and finance. If Russia wants to penetrate into African markets and stay there, it needs to set up a consistent diplomatic, political, and financial infrastructure. The point is that the Russian business needs state support to stand a higher chance in African markets. The new models of Russian-African partnership should combine national and corporate interests to benefit from state and private assets alike.

Russia and African countries are facing a new challenge as they pursue an equitable world order in line with new realities. Africans still consider Russia as one of the best allies in the international arena and as a natural counterweight to the hegemonic ambitions of a foreign power (or a group of powers). It is time for Russia to consider Africa as a strategic partner. As Mzwandile Collen Masina, Deputy Minister of Trade and Industry of South Africa, put it at the 20th Saint-Petersburg Economic forum in June 2016, "It is not risky to invest in Africa, it is risky not to invest in it".

We, Russian researchers, believe in the bright future of Africa. We are also aware that without bilateral cooperation Russia's future will not be as diverse and rich. We need each other to achieve our common objectives of genuine development. We need each other to protect our national interests. We need each other to ensure the prosperity of our peoples. We dare to hope that this conference will contribute to the expansion of horizons for Russia-Africa cooperation by providing it with a solid scientific foundation and will help Russia return to Africa without making strategic and tactical errors on its way.

Irina Abramova
Leonid Fituni

THE ECONOMIC ATTRACTIVENESS AND INVESTMENT POTENTIAL OF SUB-SAHARAN AFRICA[1,2]

In recent years, Africa has witnessed an increasing economic expansion from both old and new leading global players. Their objective is to consolidate their grip on the region, investing into current and emerging economic chains. This is the way the actors ensure the inflow of African resources for their own development under the burgeoning new world economic model. What we see today is an intense geo-economic and geopolitical scramble for Africa. The contention is about the resources of the continent, rapidly growing African markets of goods and services, intellectual potential, and the sympathy of the fastest growing population in the world[3].

What also matters is political gains, which contribute to the fruitful economic co-operation with African states, which comprise a quarter of the voting members in the UN and other international organizations. Their support in the international diplomatic arena constitutes a strategic advantage of having a loyal support group in the course of the transformation of current institutions, mechanisms, and global governance structures and amidst the shifting balance of power in the world. Penetration into African markets and an economic synergy between the Old World and Africa is possibly the only opportunity for Europe to maintain its geopolitical weight and prosperity at the level of the 20th century. China, Russia, other BRICS countries, as well as the US, are equally interested in resources and geopolitical aspects when it comes to national interests. As a result, Africa is 'a must' to co-operate with[4].

Until recently, Africa was only considered as a backward, oppressed, peripheral region. True, most countries of the continent are still lagging behind in terms of macroeconomic indicators and human development (African

---

[1] First published in *Problems of Modern Economics*. Issue 3, 2015.

[2] The article was supported by RFBR. Research project №14-07-00026 "Driving factors in the achievement of the development goals by Africa in the XXI century".

[3] Abramova I.O. *Novaja rol' Afriki v mirovoj jekonomike XXI veka* [The New Role of Africa in the World Economy in the XXI century]. Moscow, 2013. P. 5.

[4] Abramova I., Fituni L. Competing for Africa's Natural Resources. *International Affairs: A Russian Journal of World Politics, Diplomacy and International Relations*, 2009, vol. 55, no. 3, pp. 47-48.

share in the global GDP is below 2%, in global trade – below 3%, in global investment – 5%)[5]. African domestic and intergovernmental (often armed) conflicts, deepening poverty, hunger and malnutrition, and infectious deceases pushed the international community towards putting Africa high on the list of global challenges confronting humankind[6].

Yet, Africa is one of the most rapidly developing continents. Over the last 12 years, the GDP growth of Sub-Saharan Africa was second only to that of East Asia. Between 2001 and 2012, 9 Sub-Saharan economies were growing by at least 7% per year. Over the given period, the average annual growth rate of the Equatorial Guinea was over 20%, Angola – 12%, Sierra-Leone – 10%, Nigeria – 9%, Ethiopia – 8%[7]. In 2013, the annual GDP growth rate in Sub-Saharan Africa amounted to 5.2%, in 2014 – 5%. As IMF has forecasted, this indicator may fall just to 4.5% in 2015 because of declining prices for fuel and raw materials. If this overall trend continues, the Sub-Saharan growth rate will outshine the average global one (3.5%) and surpass the one of developing economies (4.3%). The IMF expects that the Sub-Saharan growth rate will hover at 5.1% in 2016[8].

Africa has focused on attracting foreign investors and creating more favourable investment climate. In 2013, foreign direct investments (FDI) in Africa amounted to $56.6 billion, in 2014 – $60.4 billion, reports UNIDO. Some estimates are that in the decade to come the active attraction of investments may add 2% more to the GDP of the continent[9]. First to penetrate the region, Western countries have now changed the manner and the matter of their rhetoric regarding the nature of economic co-operation, shifting the focus from "development aid" to "partnership" to benefit mutually from African resources and African potential. New actors are up to the par in the competition with Western economic hubs, often leaving them behind.

---

[5] Calculated on the basis of: UNCTADSTAT. UNCTAD Statistical Database. Available at: http://unctadstat.unctad.org/ReportFolders/reportFolders.aspx

[6] Abramova I.O., Fituni L.L. Jekonomika Afriki v uslovijah nadvigajushhejsja vtoroj volny mirovogo jekonomicheskogo krizisa [African economy in the context of the approaching second wave of the international economic crisis]. *Problems of Modern Economics*, 2012, no. 4, p. 107.

[7] IMF. World Economic Outlook Database, October 2012. Available at: http://www.imf.org/external/pubs/ft/weo/2012/02/weodata/weoselser.aspx?a=1&c=60 3&t=1

[8] *Regional Economic Outlook: Sub-Saharan Africa. Navigating Headwinds.* April 2015. IMF. Wash., 2015. Pp. 2-3.

[9] www.imf.org/external/np/exr/facts/rus/poorr.pdf

As for the African continent per se, over the recent two decades Sub-Saharan Africa became the economic zone which is likely to rival emerging economies (like BRICS) in terms of growth rate, role in and influence on the world economy and world politics. A number of foreign think tanks (MSCI, Economist Intelligence Unit, McKinsey, Ernst and Young) hold that Africa is getting more attractive for Western investments than China and India. As the World Bank says, the continent may be about to "take off just like China and India did 30 and 20 years ago respectively"[10]. It is no longer relevant to perceive Africa as a backward and poor continent. A lot is yet to be done but Africa, and Sub-Saharan Africa in particular, is making up the leeway[11].

The rating agency Standard and Poor's puts 8 Sub-Saharan African countries – Botswana, Ivory Coast, Ghana, Kenya, Mauritius, Namibia, Nigeria, Zambia – on a list of investment-attractive markets within the group Frontier Emerging Markets (37 countries in total), along with such other countries as Slovenia, Slovakia, Kazakhstan, Cyprus, Estonia, the United Arab Emirates.

From the 2030s onwards, Africa is forecast (by Rand, by Stanford University and by Shanghai Military University and Research Institute) to turn into the main and practically unique global strategic reserve of raw materials. First and foremost, the issue on the table is reserves of strategic and military relevance, indispensable for the military and strategic development in the 21st century. For instance, Africa's non-ferrous and rare metals are already indispensable for the production of engines for long-range bombers; the US military industrial complex imports over 50% of rare metals from SSA (DRC, Zimbabwe). Moreover, this figure for cobalt is 75%[12].

These are approximate estimates of Western analysts who explain the reasons why the leading economic world powers engaged in a "new Scramble for Africa" in the early 21st century.

Against this backdrop, Russia as a global power and an aspiring economic hub of world significance has to identify and defend its interests in Africa. Until the middle 1980s, the position of our country on the continent was quite strong. In spite of all the clichés and stereotypes bred by perestroika, the Soviet-African co-operation yielded tangible results, including huge political,

---

[10] *Ernst & Young's 2012 Attractiveness Survey*. Africa. 2012.

[11] Fituni L.L. Differenciacija razvivajushhihsja stran i novaja arhitektura mirovoj jekonomiki (voprosy teorii) [Processes of differentiation of developing countries and a new architecture of world economy (theoretical section)]. *Asia and Africa Today*, 2012, no. 10 (663), pp. 9-18.

[12] Fituni L., Abramova I. *Resource Potential of Africa and Russia's National Interests in the XXI Century*. Moscow, 2010, p. 113.

diplomatic, military and information dividend. In the 1990s, Russia lost its ground and it was not until recently that it started to recover. The latter process goes hand in hand with the recovery of the Russian economy, which badly needs much of what Africa can offer.

Russian companies, either private or state-run, have to explore Africa from scratch. They are experiencing considerable difficulties trying to enter unknown markets, and the Russian effort to regain at least some of the lost ground is hampered by competitors.

Under the circumstances, it is time for government to step in and employ political, diplomatic and other measures, and especially adjust corresponding foreign economic policies aimed at facilitating Russian investment in SSA. Consequently, it is the top priority for Russia in the region and within the new world economic development model to set up and efficiently run specialised financial institutions providing expertise and support for Russian investors in SSA.

What you really need for sensible strategic decisions regarding investments in Sub-Saharan Africa is to set criteria in order to define SSA investment attractiveness compared to the rest of the world, on the one hand, and identify the most attractive objects for investment, on the other hand. These criteria would make it possible to identify and classify areas of investments by region (sub-regions, countries, areas within the country) and industry. We came up with five basic principles of how to identify regions most attractive for investment in Sub-Saharan Africa. These are common principles of both applied (strategic investment analysis, project investment, venture capital, private equity investment analysis and valuation и country/region risk assessment) and academic (world economy, branch economies) methods and methodologies popular with most countries of the world. These principles are as follows:

• objective indicators of economic development, demographic and resource potential;

• differentiation of investment climate by different economic levels;

• investment climate of the Region is more than just the sum of investment climates in the countries of this Region (the synergy effect);

• investment climate has to be plugged into the regional economy;

• all the conditions fraught with possible risks shall be taken into consideration.

Investment decisions derive not only from the conditions of the recipient country but also from the investment strategies of Russian companies (intentions of shareholders, expertise and experience of the managing team, just to name a few). In other words, it is closely related to the very reason why investor decided to start a business and invest in SSA. We found that the best investment strategies for Russian investments in SSA are as follows:

1) The **resource-oriented investment model** implies that a Russian investor seeks to get a stable access to a strategic resource (for instance, oil, gas, aluminium, manganese, palladium, to name a few). It is a capital-intensive model with big investment and a relatively long payback period (with the payback period for the same raw material varying by project and region). Often (but not always), this strategy caters for large Russian corporations with a hefty government stake. The model can ensure Russia's access to deficit raw materials and deny these materials to rival countries.

As for geographic distribution, the model defines 4 main SSA mining areas: the Western Guinean Region (including Guinea, Sierra-Leone, Ghana, Liberia, Ivory Coast and Nigeria), the Eastern Guinean Region (Cameroon, Gabon, Equatorial Guinea, Congo-Brazzaville and the Angolan seashore), and Southern Region (the province of Sheba in the DRC and Luanda in Angola, the Copperbelt in Zambia, Zimbabwe, Botswana, Namibia, South Africa and Mozambique). A new area that is emerging in East Africa is centred on the oil reserves of South Sudan and Uganda. Judging by how active Western companies are there, Kenya and Tanzania are likely to join this area in the foreseeable future.

2) The **market-based investment model** in SSA implies that Russian investors seek to set up a stable and profitable market for their products. It could be either a market for investment products or retail trade. This model caters for large manufacturers, sales companies, wholesalers, retail chains, as well as small and middle business – especially when it comes to some specific products which are in high demand in SSA (namely water pumps, equipment for artesian wells etc.). This model can be applied in the service market as well, including IT and mobile communications – the most rapidly growing markets in SSA. To be more specific, there is a high regional demand for mobile finance and mobile payment systems, education and healthcare in remote regions in the middle of Tropical Africa.

3) **The efficiency-based investment model** with more efficient cooperative chains and business contacts. Despite the remoteness of Russia, doing business in Africa may help a company carry out specific tasks within the company's global value added chain or in terms of infrastructure. With large domestic markets, impressive GDPs, and high living standards, sub-regional economic drivers may lead this process. They boast

better business infrastructure within their geographic sub-region: Nigeria – in West Africa, Kenya – in East Africa, Ethiopia – in East and partly Central Africa, South Africa – in Southern Africa. These countries accommodate local investment headquarters, which run the expansion into neighbouring countries through local firms. The strategy goes far beyond the issues of business management and harmonisation within SSA. In many cases, corporations (investors) are eager to build an Africa-based production chain rather than export goods to the African market from Russia or other countries. Some African branches may become logistic hubs for subsidiaries in Brazil, South Africa, and India.

4) **The investment model of strategic expansion** is an economic strategy typical of particular African states or big corporations working in the national interest. For various reasons, private companies may also join the economic expansion into Africa. Such an approach requires a joint harmonized economic policy hammered out by all the actors on a mutually beneficial basis. In practice, this economic strategy for SSA is widely popular with China. Chinese state-run corporations and private companies from different industries get together in order to consolidate their grip on a particular country or branch of industry. Like China, South Africa, a would-be economic and political leader in SSA, is pursuing a similar strategy, if in a softer way.

This strategy appeals to the USA as well, yet with the tint of "market", "liberal" and "democratic" values. The USA makes effort to boost investment into and trade with SSA by means of President's initiatives, namely the Doing Business in Africa Campaign, Africa US Initiative and AGOA (just to name a few). Their purpose is to expand strategically and outpace competitors on the African market.

Each and every one of the investment models mentioned above is characterised by its own: a) set of actions; b) criteria mix, which define investment attractiveness. Whereas some of the criteria are true for all the strategies (let us call them universal), the others relate to just one of the strategies. When considering investing in a particular country, decision-makers examine criteria verifiable through statistical, macroeconomic, and expert analysis.

Basic criteria for all the investment models are as follows:

1. Macroeconomic situation and economic dynamics in the country (branch of industry): unbiased assessment of the economic potential of the object on the table;

2. Economic regime, need for investments, untapped potential, competitive environment;

3. Legal regime, taxes, business infrastructure; preferred investment, priority development areas which are supposed to attract investments; investment risks. The assessment of these factors is based on the analyses of legal factors (terms of investment in different branches, legal framework, investment protection mechanisms and their scope), political factors (legitimacy of local authorities, power balance between political groups and parties), social, economic, and environmental risks;

4. Human factor in business stands for human resources, human capital, qualified personnel, social challenges, specific features of business environment, i.e. national corporate culture and ethics, possibility of abuse, ethnic and religious factors which may determine the success of the project.

5. Country risks, including the danger of social collapse, coup d'état, internal or border military conflicts, tribal differences.

Specific criteria which fit individual business models are as follows:

For the Resource-oriented investment model:

• natural reserves (mineral, water, land, forest, fish, recreational and other resources to be developed and exploited);

• reserves of raw materials to be transported and sold on the foreign market etc.;

• geographical position and how far this region is from the state borders;

• production infrastructure;

• travel corridors, border-straddling terminals, oil pipeline, gas pipelines, distance from industrial centres;

• congenial economic-geographical location (so that investor could gain the cutting-edge in market communications and take preventive actions in investment field);

• labour potential, education and sex-age structure, infection rate and social problems;

• natural resources legislation;

• environmental laws and encumbrances.

For the Market-based investment model:

• the size of the target market (internal, border, sub-regional, regional);

• purchasing power of the population, effective demand of potential consumers;

• the size of consumer market, retail turnover and service turnover;

• specific features of target consumers (income, sex-age structure, consumption preferences);

• marketing and advertising costs aimed at shaping and boosting consumer demand, brand-new products, producibility for a region and local consumers, local traditions adding to or thwarting sales of products and services;

• smoothly-running marketing and sales system and/or the opportunity to set them up "from the scratch".

For the Efficiency-based investment models with more efficient production chains and business contacts:

• best choice of the county/city as an economic hub attractive for investment and business;

• communication and other required infrastructure[13], scientific and engineering potential, i.e. the number of experts in respective spheres and R&D expenditure (per capita);

• the level of contacts with target countries (neighbouring African countries and the EU, the US, Brazil, India, etc.);

• language, visa, tribal, caste barriers which could hinder the model implementation.

For the Expansion-based investment model:

• political, legal, institutional, military, ideological, religious, civilisational, social, cultural, propaganda levers, mechanisms, institutions which make it possible to put the strategy into practice.

For all the investment models mentioned above, the main criteria is whether SSA fits in global trends, including GDP growth rate and investment growth rate, total amount of investments, their structure and geographical distribution. These trends show that international investors are highly interested in SSA.

Sustainable FDI growth is the most indicative criterion that speaks for the investment attractiveness in SSA. This trend will remain in the decades to come to the mutual interest of all the sides. With FDI in SSA mostly allocated to long-term mining projects, there is a trend towards diversification of investments. Thus, other sectors such as export industries, food production, construction and construction materials, ad services, including mobile services and Internet, are getting to the fore[14].

In recent decades, China has become the biggest foreign investor, although the EU and the US still retain their positions due to their accumulated

---

[13] Polikanov D., Abramova I. Africa and ICT: a Change for Breakthrough? *Information Communication and Society*, 2003, vol. 6, no. 1, pp. 42-43.

[14] Abramova I., Polikanov D. Afrika v vek informacionnyh tehnologij: vozmozhnost' proryva [Africa in the century of information technology: the possibility of breakthrough]. *Asia and Africa Today*, 2001, no. 8, p. 19.

investments. In 2013, Chinese investment grew by 44% to amount to over $30bn. The year 2009 marked the point at which Chinese investment overtook American one, which made China Africa's biggest trade partner. In 2013, the African trade turnover with China amounted to over $210bn, which is 2.5 as much as that with the US. In 2013, the trade turnover between Russia and Africa constituted a mere $12bn. Over the recent years, the figures for Russia have been growing gradually, if slowly. Yet, Russia cannot rival China, India, the US, France, Italy and even Brazil in this regard. Russia provides different types of aid for African countries. Thus, for instance, it has recently written off $20bn in debts. Some Russian companies (Rostec, Lukoil, Alrosa, Rosneft, Evraz, just to name a few) have already settled down in Africa. Nonetheless, Russian investments in Africa are 10 times smaller than these of some other countries, be it annual investments and accumulated investments ($3bn) alike[15].

Present and potential Russian investors in SSA will be confronted with stiffer competition in the region and are in a desperate need for targeted and harmonized state support, the one their competitors get from respective states. Lacking in experience and unable to rely on the government support, Russian investors are doomed to make mistakes in SSA, which is bound to inflict heavy losses and damage the image of Russian business in Africa, as well as that of Russia as a whole.

From 2010 onwards, the situation with the Russian FDI in Africa is rather ambiguous. On the one hand, the big Russian companies presently operating in Southern and West Africa (Rusal, Renova, Lukoil) are going through operational difficulties due to inconsistent policies of the local authorities and excessive expectations of the Russian shareholders. On the other hand, until recent times the Russian business was building up its activities in the mining industries across the African continent. In 2011, considering Africa as an alternative to the US market it had to withdraw from, Severstal acquired a number of mining assets in three countries of West Africa.

So far, Renova has invested nearly $400mln the South African manganese industry (companies UMK and Transalloys)[16], but is currently struggling to organize production process under rather volatile conditions. Time and again did Rusal found itself on the verge of losing the aluminous plants in Guinea and Nigeria when the local authorities were about to reconsider the terms of the sales.

---

[15] www.vestifinance.ru/articles/29853
[16] http://www.kommersant.ru/doc/2115011

Let us focus on some of the graphic cases[17].

South Africa. It has been almost 20 years since the apartheid regime fell into pieces and the democratic government representing the will of the majority came to power. Ironically, this drove a wedge between South Africa (SA) and Russia. The reason for this was that, following the collapse of the Soviet Union, the Russian authorities reduced the number of Russian contacts with the African states and national liberation movements. This was a short-sighted move, which had no grounds behind it. It was not until the middle 2000s that the situation started changing for the better. This is the reason why it does not make sense to refer to our old friendship – it does not work when dealing with business partners and it may even cause resignations of young politicians and businessmen.

Another concern is that Russian businesses may break their promises and ignore their commitments, which brings damage to all the Russian companies eager to operate on the South African market. Representatives of South African business establishment state that they do not want to tolerate Russian companies which come, make commitments, and then disappear, letting down their local SA partners. Save for some rare cases, Russian businessmen are not ready for long-term co-operation with African partners. What is typical for them is a one-time investment project in pursuit of a windfall profit, and then they leave the market for good. South Africans, especially blacks, are very sensitive when they see any sign of paternalism and arrogance from the side of white foreigners, blissfully ignorant of SA history and SA achievements in science and engineering and treating their SA partners as representatives of a mediocre African country.

You will never be a partner for a SA company unless you contribute to Black Empowerment by setting up joint enterprises together with "black" SA companies. If you do so, such companies will be in charge of relations with local authorities. If you try approaching local authorities on your own, you will draw a blank and get nothing but piecrust promises and a waste of money. SA is widely known for its strict environmental law and water resources protection. If you break this law, you may be subjected to a high fine or other punitive measures, which can inflict heavy losses to the company or even force it to leave the country. It is cheaper and easier to be environmentally-friendly from

---

[17] Information on the business climate in the country and case studies was collected as a result of economic studies, sociological opinion polls and interviews within the fieldwork under the guidance of Abramova I. and Fituni L. in respective countries in 2007-2014.

the very beginning so that you do not have to spend even more later and make excuses after facing scandalous charges pressed by environmental agencies.

Zambia. KamAZ, a Russian giant, made an abortive attempt to penetrate into the Zambian market. It is said to have been a failure because it wanted "to make 300% profit from the very beginning". Another concern is that there are no direct flights between Russia and Zambia (the local office of Aeroflot was shut down several years ago).

Angola. Since 1990, the Russian company Alrosa has been developing the Angolan field "Catoca", whose reserves are estimated to be as big as 70 million carats, and the project "Luo", the biggest project on the development of kimberlite pipes "Camachiya" and "Camajicu", each of which can rival "Catoca". In the end, the "Catoca" project turned out to be a success story, whereas in the "Luo" project the company ended up freezing $120m[18].

Even though the African continent is a land of opportunity for Russian giants like Lukoil and Gazprom and small and medium businesses alike, just a handful of Russian companies managed to succeed in Africa.

In sum, there could be identified 9 common reasons for the failure of Russian companies in Africa:

1. Russian businessmen are ignorant of the political and economic situation in African countries, their investment climate, investment laws. As a result, they make the wrong choice of country and the object for investment. They lack in knowledge of specific local features and cannot build communication with local partners and local population;

2. Specifically, they are not aware of the real political situation, economic development, social, ethnic and confessional demographic structure; in most cases they have a very basic understanding of the investment law, local business customs and traditions, etc.;

3. They are reluctant to invest long-term, but are in pursuit of immediate windfall profit before winding up;

4. They lack state and corporate (through association of investors) support; they take a leap in the dark and extrapolate their experience in other countries of SSA;

5. They are ignorant of the present expertise of African specialists and their experience with Western partners;

6. They are reluctant to approach African professional and official intermediaries;

---

[18] *Kommersant Vlast'.* 04.02.2013, no. 4 (1009).

7. They do not honour their commitments and treat the local population in an arrogant manner;

8. They pay no heed to tribal chiefs who can veto any deal or, conversely, support it;

9. They bear no social responsibility (new jobs for the local population, personnel training, road construction, schools, hospitals).

In theory, the Russian investment models that would take into consideration the 9 aforementioned items could be considered successful. One should certainly bear in mind that every investment project is unique in some way, with the success or failure deriving from a mix of the African investment climate and other external factors and, more importantly, own decisions and actions of the Russian investor.

An analysis of the financial flows in 1970–2014 shows that the African market experiences "ebbs" and "flows" of long-term investments, triggered by market fluctuations. Since speculative capital accounts for a hefty share, Africa depends heavily on the world economic cycle and global stock exchanges. Capital invested in Africa is often of short-term and speculative nature, with the stock exchange being a transit point. It is also invested in short-term projects to privatize state property at an inadequate, low price.

The average return on investment is higher in Africa than in other regions. Thus, electricity production makes an average profit of 13–15% per year, with the figures for telecommunications in the range of 20–25%[19]. However, foreign capital does not abound in most SSA countries due to the risk of losing it fully or partly due to political and economic disturbances.

For all the stereotypes, amidst the global slowdown Africa turned out to be the most profitable stock market, with the highest average annual return (+10.3%) and the smallest fall (-17.3%) over the last year of the stock crisis. Africa also happened to be the market with the lowest investment risk (Beta coefficient), similar to "safe heavens" of Japan and Arab countries. At that time, the Beta coefficient for Russia was 1.5, i.e. 1.5 times as high as the world average[20].

Shares of companies in the largest African countries, namely Nigeria, Egypt, Kenya, and South Africa, are quoted low just because Western inves-

---

[19] Sukhorukov D.B. *Strahovanie investicionnyh riskov v Afrike*. Diss. kand. ekon. nauk [Insurance of investment risks in Africa. Dr. Diss. (Econ.)]. Moscow, 2007, p. 18.

[20] Ibid.

tors have to bring their money home to cover the losses. Market capitalisation in Africa amounts approximately to $400bn, which is equal to the value of Exxon Mobil. The shares of all SA companies cost as much as 60% of the rest of SSA[21].

For historical reasons, funds came to SSA as Official Development Assistance (ODA), not FDI, which reduced opportunities for state and private insurance companies. Presently, the situation is changing, but development assistance is still the main source of funds for most poor countries.

Many African countries which receive development assistance are net capital exporters: sources of dividend payments, note payments, and illegal capital outflow. However, the situation may change for the better in the following way: as developed countries focus on target investment and conditional credits, the capital outflow from Africa may reduce.

The bulk of short-term and long-term investments go into those countries which boast not just diverse mineral resources but developed infrastructure, high-skilled personnel, innovative potential. In other words, money is invested in the industries where risks have already been minimised. A case in point here is Nigeria, with developed infrastructure in oil production. The highly developed stock exchange testifies to low political risks, which ensures long-term investment of "good quality", with South Africa, Egypt, and Algeria being graphic examples.

Analysis of investment risks in SSA reveals as follows:

Russian investors face the risk that the value of assets (investments) will drop dramatically since the market is too small; they are aware of neither specific accounting and book-keeping features, nor audit standards, nationalisation, expropriation, punitive tax rates, economic conflicts, political changes, and diplomatic issues. Let alone threats and dangers which are not usually considered as investment risks: different approaches in asset evaluation, low liquidity, legal issues, activities of the governmental bodies and authorities.

For all the rapid economic growth and great opportunities, one should not forget about business risks in Africa – economic, social, and political. Among these risks are ineffective tax and monetary policy, inflation, unstable local

---

[21] Calculated in the basis of: http://www.imf.org/external/pubs/ft/weo/2013/02/weodata/weorept.aspx?sy=2010&ey=2017&scsm=1&scc=1&ssd=1&sort=country&ds=.&br=1&pr1.x=45&pr1.y=12&c=603&s=NID_NGDP&grp=1&a=1 and UN National Accounts Statistics: Main Aggregates and Detailed Tables 2011. N.-Y. 2013.

currencies, high taxes, risk of nationalization, low-skilled workers, poorly developed infrastructure, red tape.

In 2015, inflation was expected to be 7.4%, which is higher than the world average. What is more, inflation largely correlates with fluctuations in raw materials and food prices. Energy deficit, coupled with poorly-developed infrastructure and high tariffs, will also have an influence on inflation. However, according to IMF, inflation was expected to decrease from 7.4 to 6.6% in 2016[22].

African business is still stumbling on poor infrastructure, mostly in transport and energy sectors. Yet it will take some time before you get tangible results from the inflow of investments. For instance, the energy sector alone will require as much as $93bn.

Although the main indicators of the African economies are improving, the conditions for business are rather complicated. The continent is suffering from high level of corruption, low-skilled labour resources, short-sighted politics, and poor legislative framework[23]. Consequently, African countries traditionally rank low in the World Bank rating "Doing Business", although recent years have seen a positive trend. According to the rating, Mauritius, South Africa, and Botswana are the countries with the most favourable investment climate.

The main socio-economic concern in SSA is authoritarian power. However, recent years have seen some moves towards more transparent and reported administration. According to EIU research "Democracy index for countries of the world", in 2008–2014 many countries saw a lower level of democracy related to economic recession. In this regard, compared to other regions SSA experienced minor losses. In general, EIU experts conclude that the SSA economy is presently on the rise[24]. The last decade was mostly marked by positive changes, if some downturns as well. The global recession did not incur heavy losses to SSA. Possibly, SSA even benefited from recession in that investors became more interested in developing markets.

According to EIU, what could be the basis for the 6–7% economic growth in Africa is sustainable demand for raw materials in Asia, favourable demographic situation, abundant natural reserves, consistent reforms, and sustainable development. In some countries intensive reforms, political stability,

---

[22] *Regional Economic Outlook: Sub-Saharan Africa. Navigating Headwinds.* April 2015. IMF. Wash., 2015. P. 4.

[23] Fituni L.L. Mesto Afriki v postkrizisnoj mirovoj jekonomike [Africa's Place in the Post-Crisis World Economy]. *Asia and Africa Today*, 2011, vol. 1, pp. 15-20.

[24] http://www.eiu.com/public/topical_report.aspx?campaignid=AfricaInfrascope2015

democratization process, and effective management system may even lead to 8–10% growth[25].

Regarding investment risks, there is a slow but steady fall. The pace and scale, however, vary with countries, industries, and business activities, with military conflicts posing the biggest threat. Both the West and the tribal aristocracy, which is getting richer due to fruitful co-operation with foreign partners, are desperate to put an end to these conflicts. When it comes to domestic political and social conflicts, the situation is much worse, with the widening gap between the rich and the poor and the burgeoning civil society. This will also be related to modernisation, income differentiation and competition within the elite. The current task is to reform and modernise state structures, bridge gaps in legislation, in particular in equity and civil law. A special concern is the limited legal protection of the rights of investors and businessmen.

Specifically for Russian businessmen the challenge is:

– to adapt to the local sanitary and climate conditions and, what is more, to the mentality, mindset, traditions, customs, and rights of Africans; to set up friendly contacts with tribal and religious authorities;

– to honour the universal code of corporate social responsibility and contract commitments;

– to stay alert and cautious when dealing with local businessmen;

– to jettison the superstition that bribes are omnipotent on the continent.

At the same time, we believe that it is possible to overcome all these difficulties and that in the mid-term co-operation with African countries may significantly benefit Russian companies. Co-operation with African countries adds to the influence and image of Russia, reconfirming its status as a power with interests across the globe.

Recent years have seen better dynamics in Russia-Africa relations, with investment activities and trade turnover becoming more brisk. Russia wrote off the $20bn that African states had borrowed from the Soviet Union. As a result, the debt issue is practically no longer on Russia-Africa agenda.

The full potential of Russia-Africa co-operation is yet to be fully realized. In particular, this co-operation is lacking in scale, tenacity of purpose, institutional infrastructure, and respective levers to put ideas into practice.

Given the increasing role of the African factor in the international arena, it is of crucial significance for Russia to develop relations with African countries since this could strengthen the Russian position in the world politics.

---

[25] Ibid.

29

Russian diplomats had to try their best to minimize the damage incurred by the principles, forms, and conditions of co-operation based on the logic of bipolar confrontation and the Cold War doctrine. Thus, the legal framework for co-operation was adjusted, new principles were secured in conformity with new reality, as well as new directions and formats of partnership and co-operation emerged.

In spite of the shrinking trade turnover, Russia managed to retain its positive image in Africa and friendly relations with almost all African states. What is more, Russia and African states have similar opinions on the new world order, new global challenges and threats, which provides new opportunities for Russian-African co-operation in a range of spheres.

To increase the efficiency of the African track in Russian foreign policy, Russia should adjust its approaches towards a number of Africa-related challenges. First and foremost, it concerns amendments to the UN Charter pertaining to the legitimization of the right to humanitarian intervention and intervention to prevent crimes against humanity, i.e. genocide, mass extermination of civilians, etc. Although Africans have in principle approved these amendments, they take it close to heart when one intervenes into their domestic affairs ostensibly "to protect human rights and promote more radical democratic transformations". Any impulsive decisions may aggravate the internal situation in an African state which has been subjected to "humanitarian intervention", the recent events in the Ivory Coast and other states being a graphic example. This may also account for new challenges for the international community as a whole.

We personally believe that under these conditions Russia should take with a pinch of salt the decisions of the international community on international intervention into internal affairs of parties to a conflict and should develop co-operation with the African Union, sub-regional organizations, and neighbouring states, taking into account the Russian interests in the conflict countries and the international arena alike. The Russian tactics of the last decades damaged the Russian interests on the African continent for being "politically correct" and maintaining "respectability" in the eyes of the Western partners. As the global role of the developing world is on the rise, these tactics are getting more and more counterproductive. Meanwhile, the traditionally positive image of Russia in Africa rests on the fact that it offers a kind of alternative to the Western position on the continent. Thus, Russia never engaged either in slavery or in colonial partition in Africa. What is more, using political, economic and military levers, Russia actively contributed to decolonization and independent development of African countries. In this regard, the fact that Russia conducts an independent policy towards Africa, which complies with Africa's and its own interests, may condition better international image of Russia and facilitate the achievement of Russia's objectives in the region.

Dmitri Bondarenko

GLOBAL GOVERNANCE AND DIASPORAS:
THE CASE OF AFRICAN MIGRANTS IN THE USA[1]

GLOBAL GOVERNANCE AND DIASPORAS:
THEORETICAL ASPECTS OF THE PROBLEM

"Global governance" is an imperative of our times as social processes get more interrelated and interdependent under the rapid globalization the humankind is currently going through. It is not possible to tackle a mass of issues at the national level without considering the international organisations, i.e. unions of sovereign states. Clearly, we need to make joint efforts to manage global processes and settle global problems at the corresponding level – the global, transnational level, the level of global governance. It comes as no surprise that a number of scholars expect "global government" to emerge in the relatively near future[2, 3, 4, 5, 6].

Unprecedented transnational and transcontinental migration in the last decades of the 20th century and the early 21st century gives a true view from above of globalization. This phenomenon is a graphic example of globalisation, not only its key example but also a cause for an array of challenges which can only be solved by global governance. So far, however, decisions are still made at the national or, in the best case, international level. In other words, each state or each group of states (the EU, for instance) has a say[7, 8].

---

[1] First published in *World Economy and International Relations*. Issue 4, 2015.

[2] Tamir Y. Who's Afraid of a Global State? *Nationalism and Internationalism in the Post-Cold War Era.* Goldman K., Hannerz U., Westin C., eds. London, Routledge, 2000, pp. 244-267.

[3] Wendt A. Why a World State is Inevitable. *European Journal of International Relations*, 2003, vol. 9, no. 4, pp. 491-542. DOI: 10.1177/135406610394001

[4] Carneiro R.L. The Political Unification of the World: Whether, When and How – Some Speculations. *Cross-Cultural Research*, 2004, vol. 38, no. 2, pp. 162-177. DOI: 10.1177/1069397103260530

[5] Yunker J.A. *Political Globalization: A New Vision of Federal World Government*. Lanham, University Press of America, 2007. 430 p.

[6] Lykov A.Yu. *Mirovoe gosudarstvo kak budushchee mezhdunarodnogo soobshchestva* [Global State as the Future of International Community]. Moscow, Prospekt, 2013. 248 p.

[7] Betts A. Introduction: Global Migration Governance. *Global Migration Governance*. Betts A., ed. Oxford, Oxford University Press, 2011, pp. 1-33. P. 7, 16-19.

Meanwhile, the United Nations High Commissioner for Human Rights has already articulated the need for considering migration as an issue of global governance[9]. He was followed by other UN bodies[10] and international organizations which are desperate to respond to the migration-related challenges[11].

The truth is that the issue of global governance and migration goes far beyond migration flow and migrants' needs. Global governance sets "norms, rules, principles and procedures of decision making for states (and other transnational actors)"[12, 13]. There is no shadow of a doubt that diasporas also fall into the group of these nongovernmental "transnational actors". A diaspora stands for any group of individuals residing in countries different from the country of origin. We agree with the opinion of A. Ong that diaspora is "… an analytical concept too narrow to realise the multi-faceted nature of the most modern migration flows"[14]. In fact, not all network communities can be called diasporas but only those which help migrants to adapt themselves in the society without losing their cultural identity. Due to a plethora of various networks, tangible and intangible, such diaspora communities coexist within the country of destination and take forms of *status in statu* – "state in a state"[15]. What is more,

---

[8] Gamlen A., Marsh K. Introduction: Modes of Governing Global Migrations. *Migration and Global Governance*. Gamlen A., Marsh K., eds. Cheltenham; Northampton, Edward Elgar Publishing, 2011, pp. XIII-XXXIII.

[9] *Migration: A Global Governance Issue*. Available at: http://www.ohchr.org/EN/NewsEvents/Pages/MigrationGlobalGovernanceIssue.aspx (accessed 06.09.2014).

[10] *UN System Task Team on the Post-2015 UN Development Agenda. Global Governance and Governance of the Global Commons in the Global Partnership for Development beyond 2015. Thematic Think Piece. OCHCHR, OCHRLLS, UNDESA, UNEP, UNFPA*. Available at: http://www.un.org/en/development/desa/policy/ untaskteam_undf/thinkpieces/24_thinkpiece_global_governance.pdf (accessed 09.09.2014). P. 3, 4.

[11] *Conversations on the Global Governance of Migration. Helping to Build a Process for Achieving Global Governance*. Available at: http://www.icmc.net/ conversations-global-governance-migration (accessed 06.09.2014).

[12] Betts A. Introduction: Global Migration Governance. *Global Migration Governance*. Betts A., ed. Oxford, Oxford University Press, 2011, pp. 1-33. P. 4.

[13] Gamlen A., Marsh K. Introduction: Modes of Governing Global Migrations. *Migration and Global Governance*. Gamlen A., Marsh K., eds. Cheltenham; Northampton, Edward Elgar Publishing, 2011, p. 14.

[14] Ong A. Cyberpublics and Diaspora Politics among Transnational Chinese. *Interventions*, 2003, vol.5, no. 1, pp. 82-100. P. 87. DOI: 10.1080/13698032000049815

[15] Bondarenko D.M., Googueva E.A., Serov S.N., Shakhbazyan E.V. Afrikantsy v Moskve: osobennosti i problemy adaptatsii [Adaptation of Africans in Mos-

these network communities usually engage people from one country who live in the recipient country but keep in touch with friends, colleagues, business partners from the home country. Thus, the mission of global governance (which is yet to be addressed at the global level) is not just to control the flow of migrants, but also to design principles and guidelines for new emerging transnational actors – diasporas. "Consequently, diaspora governance forms part of bigger efforts to manage globalisation by incorporating trans-border communities into the current international system and adapting this very system to the transnational world"[16].

It goes without saying that the concept of global governance stands out, since global governance reflects all the various subjects which govern the world these days. This makes it attractive compared to a "government-centred perspective which narrows world politics down to "International Relations"[17]. It did not take too long before researchers across the globe started studying diasporas in relation to global governance. From what we know, there is only one monograph – a collective treatise edited by A. Betts and published in 2011[18]. Along with C. Koser, he managed to prove the scientific significance of this issue[19, 20, 21, 22]. A good reason to perceive Africa-US migration of the recent decades and African diasporas formed by it in the US

---

cow: Distinctive Features and Problems]. *Aziya i Afrika segodnya*, 2009, no. 10, pp. 43-47. P. 45; no. 11, pp. 38-41.

[16] Gamlen A. Diaspora Governance. Anderson B., Keith M., eds. *Migration: A COMPAS Anthology*. Oxford, COMPAS, 2014. Available at: http://compasanthology. co.uk/ diaspora-governance/ (accessed 09.09.2014).

[17] Dingwerth K., Pattberg P. Global Governance as a Perspective on World Politics. *Global Governance*, 2006, vol. 12, no. 2, pp. 185-203. P. 197.

[18] Betts A., ed. *Global Migration Governance*. Oxford, Oxford University Press, 2011. 368 pp.

[19] We believe that the collected articles edited by A. Gamlen and K. Marsh and published are another piece of evidence that in the 2000-2010s the global governance of immigration came to exist as a separate research field. The book combines articles of different authors previously published in other journals.

[20] Gamlen A., Marsh K., eds. *Migration and Global Governance*. Cheltenham; Northampton, Edward Elgar Publishing, 2011. 784 p.

[21] Betts A. Global Migration Governance – the Emergence of a New Debate. *The Global Economic Governance Programme Briefing Paper*. November 2010. Oxford, 2010. 4 p.

[22] Koser K., ed. International Migration and Global Governance. *Global Governance*, 2010, vol. 16, no. 3 (Special issue), pp. 301-422.

through the lens of global governance is that the US is the main country of destination or recipient state[23] whereas Africa is the largest region of origin or donor region[24].

GLOBAL GOVERNANCE AND AFRICAN DIASPORAS IN THE US: GENERAL ASPECTS

Although the US has been experiencing voluntary African immigration since the middle of 19th century[25, 26, 27], the number of African immigrants was insignificant for quite a while: it did not rise sharply overnight in 1965 when most legal restrictions were lifted. The dramatic increase took place in 1980-s and 1990-s[28, 29, 30]. The last three decades saw more Africans immigrating to the US than the 400-year history of slavery did[31]. The 21st century turned USA into the main country of destination for sub-Saharan Africans[32]. The influx of immigrants is still on the rise – among all immigrants in the US, the diaspora from the Sub-Saharan Africa is the most rapidly growing:

---

[23] Hollifield J.F., Hunt V.F., Tichenor D.J. Immigrants, Markets, and Rights: The United States as an Emerging Migration State. *Washington University Journal of Law and Policy*, 2008, vol. 27, no. 1, pp. 7-44.

[24] Abramova I.O. *Afrikanskaya migratsiya: opyt sistemnogo analiza* [African Migration: An Exercise in System Analysis]. Moscow, Institut Afriki RAN Publ., 2009. 354 p.

[25] First African immigrants who volunteered to come to the USA were of the Cape Verdian origin.

[26] Halter M. *Between Race and Ethnicity: Cape Verdean American Immigrants, 1860–1965*. Champaign, University of Illinois Press, 1993. XIX, 213 p.

[27]Wibault M. *L'immigration africaine aux Etats-Unis depuis 1965.*Paris, Université Paris I Panthéon-Sorbonne, 2005. 214 p. P. 13-19.

[28] Dixon D. *Characteristics of the African Born in the United States*. Available at: http://www.migrationpolicy.org/article/characteristics-african-born-united-states (accessed 11.09.2014).

[29] McCabe K. *African Immigrants in the United States.* Available at: http://www.migrationpolicy.org/article/african-immigrants-united-states (accessed 11.09.2014).

[30] Terrazas A. *African Immigrants in the United States.* Available at: http://www.migrationpolicy.org/article/african-immigrants-united-states-0 (accessed 11.09.2014).

[31] Curry-Stevens A. *The African Immigrant and Refugee Community in Multnomah County: An Unsettling Profile*. Portland, Portland State University Press, 2013. 116 p. P. 14.

[32] Capps R., McCabe K., Fix M. *Diverse Streams: Black African Migration to the United States*. Washington, Migration Policy Institute, 2012. 24 p. P. 3.

every 3 in 4 Africans in the US arrived no earlier than 1990[33], with 61% coming in the 21st century[34, 35, 36]. In 2010–2013 (over the course of 4 years) the number of African immigrants grew by 13% to reach 1.5 million people or about 4% of the people who live in the US but were born outside the country[37]. The US gets immigrants from almost all African countries; the last decade saw a trend toward a higher percentage of French-speaking Africans[38, 39, 40, 41, 42]. Nevertheless, war-torn English-speaking countries remain the main countries of origin. Let us take, for example, Nigeria, Ethiopia, Ghana, Kenya, Somalia, South Africa, Liberia, which account for 50% of Africans in America[43, 44, 45]. From 2000 onwards, Africans have been living in almost all

---

[33] Terrazas A. *African Immigrants in the United States.* Available at: http://www.migrationpolicy.org/article/african-immigrants-united-states-0 (accessed 11.09.2014).

[34] McCabe K. *African Immigrants in the United States.* Available at: http://www.migrationpolicy.org/article/african-immigrants-united-states (accessed 11.09.2014).

[35] Capps R., McCabe K., Fix M. *Diverse Streams: Black African Migration to the United States.* Washington, Migration Policy Institute, 2012. 24 p. P. 2.

[36] Zong J., Batalova J. *Sub-Saharan African Immigrants in the United States.* Available at: http://migrationpolicy.org/article/sub-saharan-african-immigrants-united-states (accessed 30.10.2014).

[37] Ibid.

[38] See eloquent ethnographic life descriptions of immigrants from French-speaking West Africa who came to New York in the 1990s – 2000s.

[39] Thomas K.J.A. What Explains the Increasing Trend in African Emigration to the U.S.? *International Migration Review*, 2011, vol. 45, no 1, pp. 3-28. DOI: 10.1111/j.1747-7379.2010.00837.x

[40] Adepoju A. *Changing Configurations of Migration in Africa.* Available at: http://www.migrationpolicy.org/article/changing-configurations-migration-africa (accessed 30.10.2014).

[41] Stoller P. *Money Has No Smell: The Africanization of New York City.* Chicago, University of Chicago Press, 2002. 232 p.

[42] Abdullah Z. *Black Mecca:The African Muslims in Harlem.* New York, Oxford University Press, 2010. VIII, 294 p.

[43] Wibault M. *L'immigration africaine aux Etats-Unis depuis 1965.* Paris, Université Paris I Panthéon-Sorbonne, 2005. 214 p. Pp. 69-77.

[44] Capps R., McCabe K., Fix M. *Diverse Streams: Black African Migration to the United States.* Washington, Migration Policy Institute, 2012. 24 p. P. 4.

[45] Zong J., Batalova J. *Sub-Saharan African Immigrants in the United States.* Available at: http://migrationpolicy.org/article/sub-saharan-african-immigrants-united-states (accessed 30.10.2014).

of the 50 states of the US[46]; with the largest share attributed to New-York, Maryland, and California – at least 100 thousand African immigrants in each[47, 48, 49]. Some 95% Africans in the USA settled down in cities, mostly in huge agglomerations, with New York and Washington coming first in terms of the number of Africans (over 100 thousand in each)[50, 51, 52, 53, 54, 55].

In 2013, a group of researchers from the Institute for African Studies of RAS launched an RFH (Russian Foundation for Humanities) – funded research project on black communities in the USA. So far two (2013 and 2014) field studies have been completed that cover six states (Alabama, Illinois, Massachusetts, Minnesota, New York and Pennsylvania); in small towns and major cities (Boston, Minneapolis, New York, Philadelphia, Chicago) alike.

[46] Wilson J. *African-Born Residents of the United States.* Available at: http://www.migrationpolicy.org/article/african-born-residents-united-states (accessed 11.09.2014).

[47] McCabe K. *African Immigrants in the United States.* Available at: http://www.migrationpolicy.org/article/african-immigrants-united-states (accessed 11.09.2014).

[48] Terrazas A. *African Immigrants in the United States.* Available at: http://www.migrationpolicy.org/article/african-immigrants-united-states-0 (accessed 11.09.2014).

[49] Zong J., Batalova J. *Sub-Saharan African Immigrants in the United States.* Available at: http://migrationpolicy.org/article/sub-saharan-african-immigrants-united-states (accessed 30.10.2014).

[50] Ibid.

[51] McCabe K. *African Immigrants in the United States.* Available at: http://www.migrationpolicy.org/article/african-immigrants-united-states (accessed 11.09.2014).

[52] Terrazas A. *African Immigrants in the United States.* Available at: http://www.migrationpolicy.org/article/african-immigrants-united-states-0 (accessed 11.09.2014).

[53] Takyi B.K., Boate K.S. Location and Settlement Patterns of African Immigrants in the U.S.: Demographic and Spatial Context. Konadu-Agyemang K., Takyi B.K., Arthur J.A., eds. *The New African Diaspora in North America: Trends, Community Building, and Adaptation.* Lanham, Lexington Books, 2006, pp. 50-67. Pp. 52-57.

[54] Reed H.E., Andrzejewski C.S. *The New Wave of African Immigrants in the United States.* Paper presented at Population Association of America 2010 Annual Meeting. Dallas, TX, April 15–17, 2010. Available at: http://paa2010.princeton.edu/papers/100606 (accessed 10.03.2013). Pp. 3, 5, 13, 22.

[55] Frazier J.W., Darden J.T., Henry N.F., eds. *The African Diaspora in the United States and Canada at the Dawn of the 21st Century.* Albany, State University of New York Press, 2010. VIII, 373 p. Pp. 109-212, 243-256, 287-325.

With the research still under way, the collected evidence can be used in this paper as well. First and foremost, the evidence shows that African newcomers in the US managed to set up diasporas, i.e. network communities mentioned above that combine citizens from one country – be it Ghana, Senegal, or Ethiopia. To put it another way, there is no united "African diaspora" (as many see it). This is how most interviewees see it. These diasporas are not homogenic and are deeply split into partly overlapping groups – ethnic, religious, social, political (on the basis of ethnic, linguistic, religious identity of migrants from different African countries). These groups co-operate with each other, with other black communities – African-Americans and individuals of Caribbean descent – and with the recipient society as a whole. What we found out and our interviewees proved is that the identity of diasporas is rather "narrowly ethnic" than "commonly African". It is home country that is the corner stone of the identity for most African migrants in their first generation.

With cutting-edge IT technology, migrant networks transcend the US borders and go global across other countries and continents. The function of these network communities is not only to keep in touch with friends, family, compatriots and business partners but also to ensure an emotional bond with motherland, its peoples and its culture. Close-knit connection with the motherland makes it possible to turn diasporas into truly global communities. "Africans epitomize a newly emerging phenomenon of transnationalism known for trans-border identity which keeps immigrants engaged in the activities of the local communities in the countries of origin and destination alike" [56, 57]. It is not an accident that diasporas are indicative of the preservation of economic, cultural, psychological bonds with the home country[58, 59]. Let me quote some interviews with immigrants who have been living in the USA for a while and have managed to find their place under the sun: "We never forget that our home is on the other side of the Atlantic Ocean"; "It

[56] Swigart L. *Extended Lives: The African Immigrant Experience in Philadelphia.* Philadelphia, Balch Institute for Ethnic Studies, 2001. 21 p. P. 3.

[57] Zeleza P. T. Diaspora Dialogues: Engagements between Africa and Its Diasporas. Okpewho I., Nzegwu N., eds. *The New African Diaspora: Assessing the Pains and Gains of Exile.* Bloomington; Indianapolis, Indiana University Press, 2010, pp. 31-60. Pp. 52-53.

[58] Butler K. Defining Diaspora, Refining a Discourse. *Diaspora*, 2001, vol. 10, no. 2, pp. 189-219. DOI: 10.1353/dsp.2011.0014

[59] Brubaker R. The "Diaspora" Diaspora. *Ethnic and Racial Studies*, 2005, vol. 28, no. 1, pp. 1-19. DOI: 10.1080/0141987042000289997

does not matter how far my motherland is; every time I recollect it is like coming back home"; "I will always have a soft spot for Ethiopia"; "I have always been and will always be Cape Verdean". The bond with the home country is deeply-entrenched in the daily routine. Thus, for instance, most families cook traditional food[60], listen to African music and watch African movies. They also celebrate important events in the same way they did at home ...[61, 62, 63].

The bottom line here is that migration is a major phenomenon of the modern globalization and this phenomenon should be subject to global governance by means of transnational regulation of migration flows and norms for foreign diasporas. On the other hand, diasporas bred by migration may be

---

[60] These days some shops sell popular African products (for instance, yam flour) grown in the USA but packaged in a typically African way.

[61] In fact, only the first generation of African immigrants in the USA pledges deep allegiance to the motherland. They have to admit that their children are born and bred "typical" Americans. Many would agree with the informant from Nigeria who said "The biggest failure in my life is that I failed to get my kids interested in Africa". A respondent from Sierra-Leone gave a clear-cut answer "Even in the families which try to instill African values, children adopt American values as well. But these are different types of values". Lots of respondents said something like "My kids are fully and truly Americans, not Nigerians. They don't have the faintest idea about Nigeria. Another graphic example is an interview with a Somalia emigrant who said "I don't think that anybody who was born here will ever get interested in what is happening in Somalia. Their identity is closely knit with the United States, they think American, they consider themselves Americans, and most of them have problems dealing with their parents. As a result, they leave parents once they turn 18. They don't even like to be called Somali. They say "Hold on, I come from Massachusetts, I am American. And why do you call me Somali?" As the researchers from the Institute for African Studies of RAS talked to young Africans living in the USA they found out that it makes sense what the first generation African immigrants had told them about the youth. As S.S. Nyang aptly put, "present African immigrants are part and parcel of the American society. As a result, their children and grandchildren will be driven by the same factors which drive other American kinds". For a deeper description of main problems between African immigrants and their children as well as the perspective of the former and the latter see [Incomplete sentence]

[62] Nyang S.S. The African Immigrant Family in the United States of America: Challenges and Opportunities. Ìrìnkèrindò: A Journal of African Migration, 2011, no. 5. Available at: http://www.africamigration.com/Issue%205/Articles/HTML/Sulayman-Nyang_The-African-Immigrant-in-the-USA.htm (accessed 19.07.2013).

[63] Swigart L. Extended Lives: The African Immigrant Experience in Philadelphia. Philadelphia, Balch Institute for Ethnic Studies, 2001. 21 p. Pp. 7-9.

seen as (or may actually be) the agents of social and political global governance. This type of governance is transnational given the way it affects societies and states of origin and those of destination. This idea is substantiated by the statistics regarding the African diaspora in the USA.

SOCIETIES OF ORIGIN

The Research Group members often came across those African immigrants who expressed their desire to come back to Africa, as well as those who have never considered such an option. Most interviewees, however, are convinced that African diasporas can and have to take an active part in the life of their homeland. One of them put it as follows: "There is no doubt that African diasporas have to affect the course of events at home. This is how I see it. I believe you have no right to forget your homeland and your peoples. You have to take every effort to serve your country". Another one told us about his experience visiting the homeland: "Whenever I come to Chad, I feel that I need to do something for it. It is where I come from". To be more specific, the respondents stated that the diaspora should make a larger contribution to economic progress by lobbying for American investments into their home countries, building up trade between home country and the USA, attracting American tourists, etc. They often pondered how the expertise and knowledge of diasporas may benefit the development of social infrastructure, healthcare and education. Not least, the respondents mentioned that diasporas should participate in the politics at home to sustain peace, build the civil society and democratic state free from corruption, red tape etc. Many consider democratic freedom to be one of the main benefits from immigration to America. These people believe that with their experience in the USA, their education, well-being and business contacts diasporas must contribute to the democratisation of society and state in the home country. As one Somali refugee from Ogaden turned American politics student put it, "if you ask me whether the diaspora should play a leading role in the political transformation and democratization of African countries, my answer will be "Yes, certainly" because it holds all the cards for this".

Some respondents do not just pay lip service to the issue of participation in the life of the homeland. They do whatever they can and sometimes they even come back to Africa to benefit their motherland with their expertise and life experience gained during their years as immigrants[64, 65]. The most popu-

---

[64] In particular, this is exactly what one respondent from Philadelphia did. A Liberian journalist who criticised authorities and had to flee the home country in 1995 due

lar way to take part in the social and political life at home is the one a Nigerian respondent mentioned, i.e. to submit a reform project to the government. Embassies and consulates are also approached, as well as the international community desperate to fight corruption. A good example here is petitions in Western newspapers[66]. It is more rarely that Africans have interest and ability to participate in economic projects. A case in point here is a respondent who invested in Kenyan energy industry together with his friends. His other friends from the Kenyan diaspora in the USA also managed to invest in Kenyan real estate, education and agriculture. Another one told us about Ethiopians in the USA who invest in their home country[67, 68].

These responses suggest that most African immigrants are focused on targets of helping specific people, i.e. family members who stayed at home. Family bonds are a corner stone in a set of African values. It is an imperative for any African, even for the educated and highly "Westernized". Given the fact that Africans prefer the concept of a big (extended) family rather than one of a small (nuclear) family, it is a hard burden to support all family members. In fact, some Africans cannot support their families at home due to the current economic situation, lack of skills or education. And this is exactly the reason why they go abroad. The life of an immigrant, in America and elsewhere, is full of hardship and you have to work hard. This is why only a few immigrants want their family members to follow the lead and come to

---

to political persecution made a comeback in the summer 2014 and became Head of Department in a Liberian College. He was desperate to help his country recover after the civil wars and authoritarian regime. Other respondents told about their friends who did the same, i.e. about Kenyans who came back to Kenya to build a career in politics and Nigerian who came home to run road construction projects.

[65]*Ìrìnkèrindò: A Journal of African Migration*, 2014, no. 7. Available at: http://www.africamigration.com/Issue%207/Compilation/issue%207%20full.pdf (accessed 18.09.2014).

[66]Wibault M. *L'immigration africaine aux Etats-Unis depuis 1965*.Paris, Université Paris I Panthéon-Sorbonne, 2005. 214 p. Pp. 176-180.

[67] First and foremost, it holds true for the most affluent representatives of the Ethiopian community in Russia.

[68] Bondarenko D.M., Demintseva E.B., Usacheva V.V., Zelenova D.A. African Entrepreneurs in Moscow: How They Did It Their Way. *Urban Anthropology and Studies of Cultural Systems and World Economic Development*, 2014, vol. 43, no. 1-3, pp. 205-254. Pp. 223, 229.

America[69, 70, 71, 72, 73]. Some deem it more reasonable to support their family rather than to help them settle down. Thus, for instance, an aged doctor who migrated to the USA about 25 years ago and is currently a professor at the Medical Department said the following: "All my family members live in Nigeria. We keep in touch every day. I go to Nigeria two or three times per year, give them money, drugs, clothes, books. But I do not recommend them to follow my example" (i.e. to immigrate).

---

[69] Africans, those who came to America recently and those who came a long time ago, often call America – *land of opportunities* compared to Africa and to Europe (among the respondents there were those who used to live in the European countries such the UK, Italy, Netherlands, Finland but left these countries for a better life in America. They believed that they stood higher chance of achieving success in the US. As noted by an engineer from Cameroon who came to the USA from Italy and turned down a job offer in France "I was led here by a feeling that if you try your best, if you are not a lazy and if you have a purpose in life, you will have a chance to get it all. This idea really works in this country, much better than anywhere else". It is the belief in the "American Dream" that led to the USA those who left their countries by their own choice. "I believe that this is the foundation of America that you can come here and achieve whatever you want", – is how a young Ugandan lady put it. Yet many respondents noted that bright prospects come with much more hardship they used to imagine". In this regard, the story of an informant from Liberia is graphic example: "Frankly speaking, it was a culture shock for me. I judged America by the movies I watched. It seemed to me that this country opens a window of opportunity; you can come here and become rich overnight. However, once you get here you find out that it is all different. You can get what you want but you have to work hard. It seems to me that for an African immigrant it is 10 times as hard". Another graphic example is the story of a Nigerian emigrant: "What led me to America? – laughing, – Dream – American Dream. In Nigeria, each and everybody want to move to America. Everybody! I tried my best for 10 years to live in America. I did whatever possible, put my heart into it. When you are in Nigeria, you hear so much good about America. Then you come there and think that it is easy-peasy to become rich. The reality is that you need to struggle all the time".

[70] Wibault M. *L'immigration africaine aux Etats-Unis depuis 1965.* Paris, Université Paris I Panthéon-Sorbonne, 2005. 214 p. Pp. 39-43

[71] Ojo-Ade F. Living in Paradise?: Africans in America. *Ìrìnkèrindò: A Journal of African Migration*, 2011, no. 4. Available at: http://africamigration.com/Articles2011/OJO%20ADE%20LIVING%20IN%20PARADISE.htm (accessed 19.07.2013).

[72] Moore A.R. *The American Dream Through the Eyes of Black African Immigrants in Texas.* Lanham, University Press of America, 2013. 120 p.

[73] Graw K., Schielke S., eds. *The Global Horizon: Expectations of Migration in Africa and the Middle East.* Leuven: Leuven University Press, 2012. 199 p.

Immigrants help their family at home in a number of ways[74, 75, 76], remittances being the main one. It holds true for all the respondents from workers at poultry farms to college professors, from hairdressers to prospering real estate agents[77, 78, 79]. "Each and every time I get my salary, I start computing how much I can send to Nigeria", acknowledges a sales assistant in the Philadelphia-based African grocery store. "I have to send money home every month. You can say to you family "Sorry, no money this month. But it is not an option for you and you keep sending money" – these are the words of a Somali interviewee with a degree in teaching. Many respondents mentioned the mandatory character of this tradition to help relatives at home. A Nigerian interviewee who runs an IT department in a big international company put it as follows: "I help my family all the time. It is very important. I help them a lot. There is no other way". A sales assistant from a computer shop from Niger made an accurate observation, calling this help to the family in Africa "sacred duty". Lots of immigrants are subjected to psychological pressure from their relatives in Africa who take for granted any help delivered by prosperous American relatives. Some respondents mentioned that they have to take three or four jobs at the same time to help family members[80, 81]. As

---

[74]Wibault M. *L'immigration africaine aux Etats-Unis depuis 1965*.Paris, Université Paris I Panthéon-Sorbonne, 2005. 214 p. Pp. 171-175.

[75]Aina T.A., Moyo B., eds.*Giving to Help, Helping to Give: The Context and Politics of African Philanthropy*. Dakar: Amalion Publishing; TrustAfrica, 2013. 464 p.

[76] Okome M.O., Copeland-Carson J., Osili U. *African Immigrant Innovations in 21st Century Giving*. Available at: http://www.academia.edu/6049546/African_Immigrant_Innovations_in_21st_Century_Giving (accessed 13.02.2014).

[77]Wibault M. *L'immigration africaine aux Etats-Unis depuis 1965*.Paris, Université Paris I Panthéon-Sorbonne, 2005. 214 p. Pp. 171-173.

[78] Curry-Stevens A. *The African Immigrant and Refugee Community in Multnomah County: An Unsettling Profile*. Portland, Portland State University Press, 2013. 116 p.

[79] Okome M.O. African Diasporas. Merz B.J., Chen L.C., Geithner P.F., eds. *Diasporas and Development*. Cambridge; London, Harvard University Press, 2007, pp. 151-184. Pp. 23, 82-83.

[80] Horst C. *Connected Lives: Somalis in Minneapolis, Family Responsibilities and the Migration Dreams of Relatives*. Geneva: United Nations High Commissioner for Refugees, 2006. 24 p. Pp. 10-13.

[81] Okome M.O. The Antinomies of Globalization: Some Consequences of Contemporary African Immigration to the United States of America. *Ìrìnkèrindò: A Journal of African Migration*, 2002, no. 1. Available at: http://www.africamigration.com/archive_01/m_okome_globalization_01.htm (accessed 19.07.2013).

G.A. Arthur put it, "strong family bonds explained by African traditional values defined the life of immigrants in America" [82].

Although remittances go to specific people in Africa, they have an effect on the society and state as a whole, constituting a major GDP share in many African countries[83, 84]. "The chances are that the remittances will be on the rise as long as the number of African immigrants in the USA is growing. Our research interests lie in the repercussions of this phenomenon" [85]. With this money transfer African governments may reduce social tensions. African countries set up special agencies to design programs on how to raise more money from successful emigrants for the benefit of social, cultural and educational national projects. These agencies also consider ways of engaging these people in the promotion of their home country, by creating its positive image abroad[86, 87]. At the same time many African states deem it necessary to build relations with the home country, with the help of embassies, consulates and diasporas per se.

RECIPIENT SOCIETY

As mentioned above, despite the rise in migration flows, Africans still constitute a modest percent of immigrants in the USA, and a very minor share in the total population of the country. Some researchers even call Africans "invisible" in the American society, which also makes them "invisible" in the intellectual discourse[88, 89]. One of the respondents made a statement

[82] Arthur J.A. *Invisible Sojourners: African Immigrant Diaspora in the United States.* Westport; London, Praeger, 2000. 216 p. P. 107.

[83] Ratha D., Mohapatra S., Özden Ç., Plaza S., Shaw W., Shimeles A. *Leveraging Migration for Africa: Remittances, Skills, and Investments.* Washington, The International Bank for Reconstruction and Development / The World Bank, 2011. XX, 212 p.

[84] According to the World Bank, in 2013 remittances of African emigrants to SSA countries amounted to $31 bln or about 2% GDP. It took them decade to (from 2003 onwards) increase sevenfold.

[85] Reed H.E., Andrzejewski C.S. *The New Wave of African Immigrants in the United States.* Paper presented at Population Association of America 2010 Annual Meeting. Dallas, TX, April 15–17, 2010. Available at: http://paa2010.princeton.edu/ papers/100606 (accessed 10.03.2013). P. 4.

[86] Gamlen A. Diaspora Governance. Anderson B., Keith M., eds. *Migration: A COMPAS Anthology.* Oxford, COMPAS, 2014. Available at: http://compasanthology. co.uk/diaspora-governance/ (accessed 09.09.2014).

[87] Gamlen A. Why Engage Diasporas? *ESRC Centre on Migration, Policy and Society.Working Paper No. 63.* Oxford, University of Oxford, 2008. 17 p. Pp. 6-9.

[88] Arthur J.A. *Invisible Sojourners: African Immigrant Diaspora in the United States.* Westport; London, Praeger, 2000. 216 p.

that "there is more awareness of Africans these days. It is true that, as far as Africa and Africans are concerned, people are still impolite. But it is not weird and awkward any more to be an African in America". In any case, one way or another, Africans also shape the basic principles of public life and state politics (domestic and foreign alike) in both countries of origin and the recipient country i.e. the USA.

It further substantiates the idea that political actors mould the norms and rules of global government not on their own, but in tandem with the globalising civil society, its institutions and organisations[90, 91]. A case in point here is recent public debate on the immigration policy among the American establishment, including President B. Obama. They discussed how to help immigrants to integrate into the society and how to build relations with countries of origin. These debates were triggered by the Washington Summit of the US and African leaders which took place 4-6 August 2014[92, 93]. Remarkably, African immigrants in America also took the floor and blamed the government for turning a blind eye to their needs and problems. They also encouraged the political establishment to take into account their interest while designing immigration reforms[94, 95, 96]. Some of the respondents also expressed

---

[89]Hintzen P.C., Rahier J.M., eds. *Problematizing Blackness: Self-Ethnographies by Black Immigrants to the United States.* New York; London, Routledge, 2003. 210 p.

[90] Castells M. The New Public Sphere: Global Civil Society, Communication Networks, and Global Governance. *The Annals of the American Academy of Political and Social Science*, 2008, vol. 616, no. 1, pp. 78-93. DOI: 10.1177/0002716207311877

[91] Fries T., Walkenhorst P. *Sharing Global Governance: The Role of Civil Society Organizations.* Gütersloh, Bertelsmann Stiftung, 2011. 60 p.

[92]*Remarks by the President at Press Conference After U.S.–Africa Leaders' Summit.* Available at: http://www.whitehouse.gov/the-press-office/2014/08/06/remarks-president-press-conference-after-us-africa-leaders-summit (accessed 13.09.2014).

[93]*Serrano Applauds First-Ever U.S.–Africa Leaders' Summit, Stresses Importance of Immigration Reform for the Region.* Available at: http://serrano.house.gov/press-release/serrano-applauds-first-ever-us-africa-leaders-summit-stresses-importance-immigration (accessed 13.09.2014).

[94]*African Immigrant Recommendations on the U.S.–Africa Leaders' Summit.* Available at: http://press.org/events/african-immigrant-recommendations-us-africa-leaders-summit (accessed 13.09.2014).

[95] Babalwaiz A.Y. *Backdrop of US–Africa Leaders' Summit: Anger over Obama's Neglect of African Immigrants Priorities.* Available at: http://www.applauseafrica.com/xchange/382-backdrop-of-us-africa-leaders-summit-anger-over-obama-s-neglect-of-african-immigrants-priorities (accessed 13.09.2014).

concern about the integration of Africans (and all the newcomers in general) into the American society and their readiness to find a solution. Thus, for instance, a well-educated Liberian who has been living in the US since the late 1980s told us that one of the reasons she teaches adults is that "I must fight for the rights of immigrants to integrate into the society". It is essential that the immigration policy prove that "domestic policy of one state may constitute an implicit form of global governance" as a weight to keep other states under control[97].

In fact, there is one more reason why African immigrants are getting less "invisible" in the American society. It is not just due some tragic notorious events. The point is that Africans in the USA are well-educated compared to other immigrants. Africa is suffering from the "brain drain". There are several reasons for this, i.e. immigrants pursue a better life, most African alumni are reluctant to leave America after graduation, and many refugees and political emigrants are high-class professionals[98, 99, 100, 101, 102, 103]. Statistics show

---

[96]*Include Immigration Reform on the Agenda of the White House's US–Africa Leaders' Summit, Slated for August 2014 in DC.* Available at: http://www.change. org/p/president-of-the-united-states-include-immigration-reform-on-the-agenda-of-the-white-house-s-us-africa-leaders-summit-slated-for-august-2014-in-dc (accessed 13.09.2014).

[97] Betts A. Introduction: Global Migration Governance. Betts A., ed. *Global Migration Governance.* Oxford, Oxford University Press, 2011, pp. 1-33. Pp. 7, 22, 26.

[98] Thomas K.J.A. What Explains the Increasing Trend in African Emigration to the U.S.? *International Migration Review,* 2011, vol. 45, no. 1, pp. 3-28. DOI: 10.1111/j.1747-7379.2010.00837.x

[99] Reynolds R.R. An African Brain Drain: Igbo Decisions to Immigrate to the US. *Review of African Political Economy,* 2002, vol. 29, no. 92, pp. 273-284. DOI: 10.1080/03056240208704613

[100] Hagopian A., Thompson M.J., Fordyce M., Johnson K.E., Hart L.G. The Migration of Physicians from Sub-Saharan Africa to the United States of America: Measures of the African Brain Drain. *Human Resources for Health,* 2004, vol. 2, no. 17. DOI: 10.1186/1478-4491-2-17. Available at: http://www.human-resources-health.com/content/2/1/17 (accessed 18.09.2014).

[101] Okome M.O., Banoum B.N.-N. Dimensions of African Migration to the United States: Labor, Brain Drain, Identity Formation and Naturalization. *Ìrìnkèrindò: A Journal of African Migration,* 2004, no. 3. Available at: http://www.africamigration. com/archive_03/FINAL%20EDIT%20EDITORIAL.htm (accessed 19.07.2013).

[102] Lobo A.P. Unintended Consequences: Liberalized US Immigration Law and the African Brain Drain. Konadu-Agyemang K., Takyi B.K., Arthur J.A., eds. *The New*

that Africans rank first among other immigrant communities in terms of education. They do even better than whites, let alone African-Americans[104]. "...the US, Canada and Australia attract a hefty share of well-educated Africans whereas the less educated opt for the UK, France and other EU countries" [105]. And a number of well-educated Africans who managed to prosper and gain high position in the society are ready to help out immigrants from African countries and to speak up for them at the local and national level.

They make every effort and do it in different ways to show us that "governance of diaspora is a multi-level process covering, international, national and local institutions and processes" [106]. Thus, for instance, 18-24 June 2014 in Massachusetts saw "the African week" convened by those willing to "make people hear the African voice in Massachusetts" [107]. 19 October 2014, New-York hosted the 8th annual African parade and festival with the motto "Let's raise our voice all together to strengthen the power of our communities" [108]. It is more often than not that funds and participation come from communities of African women, entrepreneurs and professionals (doctors, lawyers just to name a few), i.e. people from the same country

African Diaspora in North America: Trends, Community Building, and Adaptation. Lanham, Lexington Books, 2006, pp. 189-208.

[103]Kaba A.J. Africa's Migration Brain Drain: Factors Contributing to the Mass Emigration of Africa's Elite to the West. Okpewho I., Nzegwu N., eds. *The New African Diaspora: Assessing the Pains and Gains of Exile.* Bloomington; Indianapolis, Indiana University Press, 2010, pp. 109-123.

[104] Logan J. R. Who Are the Other African Americans? Contemporary African and Caribbean Immigrants in the United States. Shaw-Taylor Y., Tuch S.A., eds. *The Other Americans: Contemporary African and Caribbean Immigrants in the United States.* New York, Rowman & Littlefield Publishers, 2007, pp. 49-68. Pp. 55-56.

[105] Capps R., McCabe K., Fix M. *Diverse Streams: Black African Migration to the United States.* Washington, Migration Policy Institute, 2012. 24 p. P. 1.

[106] Gamlen A. Why Engage Diasporas? *ESRC Centre on Migration, Policy and Society.Working Paper No. 63.* Oxford, University of Oxford, 2008. 17 p. P. 6.

[107]*"Africa Week" Proclamation by Governor Deval Patrick of Massachusetts.* Available at: http://www.tadias.com/06/09/2014/africa-week-proclamation-by-governor-deval-patrick-of-massachusetts/ (accessed 19.09.2014).

[108]*African Day Parade and Festival.* Available at: http://www.africandayparade.org/ (accessed 09.11.2014).

or of the same ethnicity[109, 110, 111]. Such unions, either registered or informal, either seeking to encompass all the USA or seeking to cater for the needs of Africans in one particular city or even district[112, 113], become new cells of American civil society and, consequently, have a bearing on the society and governmental bodies alike.

Our special interest was small, local organisations, self-proclaimed spokesmen of Africans from all countries[114, 115, 116]. They may, however, be dominated by any particular diaspora, a diaspora the founder came from. In such cases many are desperate to overcome the differences between African

---

[109] Organizations often unite people on the basis of several factors, i.e. people of the same profession and from the same country or compatriots living in the same region (*Association of Ghanaian Lawyers in America, Zambians in Atlanta* etc.).

[110] Ogbaa K. *The Nigerian Americans*. Westport, Greenwood Press, 2003. 200 p. Pp. 81-96.

[111] Abbott C.W. Nigerians in North America: New Frontiers, Old Associations? Konadu-Agyemang K., Takyi B.K., Arthur J.A., eds. *The New African Diaspora in North America: Trends, Community Building, and Adaptation*. Lanham, Lexington Books, 2006, pp. 141-165.

[112] For instance, from the middle 1980s to 2000s Philadelphia saw 40 new organizations of African ethnic groups or Africans in general. A relatively small city of Columbus (the Ohio State) accommodates over a dozen of associations of migrants from Ghana based on ethnicity or profession.

[113] Agbemabiese P. *The Changing "Face" of African Immigrants and Refugees: The Case of Ghanaian Immigrants in Columbus, Ohio*. Available at: https://www.academia.edu/1530113/The_Changing_Face_of_African_Immigrants_an d_Refugees_The_Case_of_Ghanaian_immigrants_in_Columbus_Ohio (accessed 20.10.2012).

[114] Among organisations which heads and members talked to the researchers from the Institute for African studies are as follows: *African Cultural Alliance of North America* (with branches in Philadelphia, the most densely populated city in Pennsylvania, and Maryland), *Africans in Boston*, as well as *African–American Friendship, Inc.* in Boston, *Panafrican Association* in Chicago just to name a few. There are also smaller organisations, like the one studied by G. Copeland-Carson in Minneapolis, which seek to unite black people from one city or, at least, from one district – *neighbourhood*.

[115] Copeland-Carson J. *Creating Africa in America: Translocal Identity in an Emerging World City*. Philadelphia, University of Pennsylvania Press, 2004. 256 p.

[116] Copeland-Carson J. "Africa" in Minnesota: New Models of Translocal Culture. *Ìrìnkèrindò: A Journal of African Migration*, 2011, no. 4. Available at: http://www.africamigration.com/Articles2011/COPELAND-CARSON%20AFRICA %20IN%20MINNESOTA.htm (accessed 07.03.2013).

diasporas (differences often "imported from Africa") for the common good. Jointly together they try to settle the problems of individuals and groups alike. The active members of these groups believe that the best way to achieve these objectives is to co-operate with authorities and affect their work. "We talk to mayor candidates and candidates for the members of the municipal council," interviewees told us, "and we do this because we want these people to follow our rules in exchange for our votes." Thus, for instance, the Association *"Africans in Boston"* seeks to "strengthen the African electorate in the region and to raise its political status" and "to provide Africans and their friends with a platform to bridge cultural, education and professional gaps between African diasporas". What is more, African immigrants have to be aware of their common political objectives. It is the only way to overcome "the isolation and weakness of African diasporas"[117].

* * *

All in all, evidence on the African immigrants in the USA shows that diasporas constitute both objects (or, to be more precise, may become objects) and real subjects of global governance. They have a bearing on the social life, domestic and foreign politics in both the countries of origin and the recipient country i.e. the USA. They contribute to the principles and mechanisms which govern global processes. This contribution, if modest, is beyond doubt a significant one.

---

[117]*Africans in Boston.* Available at: http://africansinboston.org/about-us/mission/ (accessed 14.09.2014).

Tatyana Denisova

THE "WAVE OF DEMOCRATISATION"
AND ELECTORAL PROCESSES IN SUB-SAHARAN AFRICA[1]

The "wave of democratisation" that engulfed Africa in the 1990s-2000s led Russian and foreign political scientists, who for many years had been studying the evolution of authoritarian regimes in the African context but who suddenly found themselves facing a whole new reality – the multidimensional political changes that had taken place in most countries of the continent, to start re-searching the root causes and the essence of these changes. One of the key manifestations of the "democratisation" is that a number of countries held par-liamentary and presidential elections. However, the question arises of whether we can really call these processes "democratisation". Does the power of new African regimes derive from their peoples? After all, real democracy presup-poses not just the very fact of holding parliamentary and presidential elections, but also a penalty for falsifying their results, as well as a system of checks and balances that limits the power of an elected leader.

In nearly all tropical African countries presidential, parliamentary, guber-natorial, and local elections have become a familiar feature of political life. If observers do not identify serious violations during elections, they are deemed legitimate, and the society with a new leader or the same old one continues along the path of democratisation. At the same time, it is not taken into ac-count that in the African context elections may become a matter of life or death for candidates and their voters, as participants often resort to violent methods of protecting their electoral interests. As a result, there emerges the phenomenon aptly called "democrazy"[2] by British researcher Paul Collier, and which in Russian literature is usually referred to as "guided democracy", "quasi-democracy", or "pseudo-democracy"[3].

In Africa, the emergence of pseudo-democracy has usually been preceded by a regime of personal management (authoritarianism) or military dictator-ship. The power of authoritarian leaders was based on personal charisma, political patronage (the use of a significant part of public resources and posi-

---

[1] First published in *Journal of the Institute for African Studies.* Issue 1, 2015.
[2] Collier P. *Wars, Guns, and Votes.* N.-Y., 2009, p. 15.
[3] *Sovremennaja Afrika: metamorfozy politicheskoj vlasti* [Modern Africa: the Me-tamorphosis of Political Power]. Moscow, 2009.

tions to reward supporters and relatives of the regime leader), repression (persecution of opposition), total control of security forces over political and private life of citizens, and specific ideologies – Mobutism in Democratic Republic of Congo (DRC), Ujamaa socialism in Tanzania, Zambian humanism in Zambia, etc.

After the end of the Cold War, it was no longer necessary to finance dictatorial regimes in order to maintain them as allies in the struggle between the two military-political blocs. Accordingly, foreign governments, financial institutions, and humanitarian organisations started demanding that African leaders carry out democratic reforms in exchange for material assistance. However, the external pressure often produced opposite results: not all rulers were ready to do something against their will, and some turned out to be surprisingly resourceful in finding ways to avoid this.

In the meantime, by the 1990s, the most far-sighted politicians in the majority of African countries had realised the need for serious political change and the creation of at least an appearance of moving towards democratisation. As a result, despite the high cost of holding elections and the risk of unfavourable outcomes, only paranoid dictators, such as, for example, Macias Nguema in Equatorial Guinea, avoided elections. First of all, this was due to the fact that both politicians and voters were ready for or insisted on holding them. For the opposition it was a possible path to power, for the ruling party – a way to legitimise power in the eyes of citizens and foreign donors. Voters were satisfied because through the election process they could voice their opinion, get involved in the political process, participate in mass action, etc.

Meanwhile, many of the incumbent leaders, who had been quite confident of their position, unexpectedly did not get the vote they anticipated. Often they bore the brunt of their own ignorance: surrounded by sycophants, the rulers were not able to assess the mood of the electorate. This primarily concerned the longest-serving rulers, who had stayed in power for 20–30 years or more and lost the touch with reality. At least one leader has fallen victim to this: Kenneth Kaunda (Zambia), who let the citizens vote because he did not doubt his victory. As a result, in 1991 he received only about 20% of the vote. Indeed, a certain part of the population did support the old president, especially in his native region, where he spent large sums on public needs. Naturally, Kaunda was outraged by the "ingratitude" of Zambians. Later he went on a "tour" of African capitals, advising the rulers not to repeat his mistake – not to hold elections if the results were unpredictable.

Many leaders agreed to amending the constitution by setting a two-term limit for election to the office of head of state, believing that before the end of their terms they would have time to make another amendment to the main law of the country. In fact, Nigerian President O. Obasanjo (1999–2007) tried but failed to extend his term in 2007[4], just like Zambian President Frederick Chiluba (1991–2002) in 2000[5]. However, Chadian and Ugandan presidents – Idris Debi and Yoweri Museveni – did succeed in this.

In principle, a democratic election is considered to be the main condition for the legitimisation of a ruler, who is thereby bestowed the right to act on the promises he made during his election campaign. In case he succeeds in implementing the declared programme, he is able to confidently confront the opposition, which cannot legitimately challenge the policy of a legitimate government. This should also help reduce the level of violence: even if irreconcilable opponents of the regime do not recognize the legitimate government's right to pursue its policies, they find it difficult to gather mass support for violent actions, since they cannot claim that their struggle is just.

Yet democracy does not always create conditions for the consolidation of peace and stability. "Democratisation" in Africa has evoked general enthusiasm, both on the continent and beyond, but the process has turned out to be much more complex and controversial. Often "democratisation" in developing countries produces the effect opposite to what is observed in developed countries, because competitive elections reignite inter-tribal, inter-confessional, and inter-factional contradictions, which languished or were suppressed by authoritarian rulers, sometimes leading to violence. That is, in developed societies democratisation facilitates the strengthening of political stability, while in developing ones it aggravates the already existing preconditions for instability.

As an example of political destabilisation against the backdrop of democratisation, we can point to the deterioration of the domestic political situation in Nigeria after the 2011 elections, which, according to Western observers, were not accompanied by serious violations. However, they led to an aggravation of the contradictions between the Muslim North of the country (dissatisfied with the victory of Goodluck Jonathan, a Christian) and the Christian South, and to the revitalisation of the armed Islamist sect Boko Haram[6].

---

[4]*Nigerija. Spravochno-monograficheskoe izdanie* [Nigeria. Reference book]. Moscow, 2013, p. 105.

[5]*Zambija. Spravochno-monograficheskoe izdanie* [Zambia. Reference book]. Moscow, 2013, p. 118.

[6] Denisova T.S. Ot Majtacine do Boko Haram [From Maitatsine to Boko Haram]. *Vostok (Oriens)*, 2014, vol. 4, pp. 70-82.

In developed countries the necessity to implement voter-approved policies does discipline rulers, especially since all their actions are monitored by the media, non-governmental organisations, the opposition, etc. If they are seen to advance their own interests or harm public ones, most likely they will not be re-elected, or will be – but only in the absence of worthy contenders. In Tropical Africa, where the achievements of a leader in the social and economic spheres are of less importance than the effectiveness of the patronage system he has created, it is the scale of the outreach of this system that will largely determine the outcome of the election. In turn, the struggle for access to patronage resources contributes to even greater public disengagement and the rise of violence.

Politicians, both Western and African, tend to strive for gaining and maintaining power. Above all because politics is their vocation and "profession". However, in African countries, to a much greater extent than anywhere else, power means obtaining almost unlimited opportunities for self-enrichment, including at the expense of state coffers. How else to explain the desire of elderly presidents (K. Kaunda, F. Houphouet-Boigny, etc.) to hold onto their position even despite the risk of being overthrown and killed in the office, as it happened, for example, with M. Nguema in 1978 or with Liberian President W. Tolbert in 1980?

An important factor, which often predetermines the outcome of an election, remains the tribal affiliation of the candidate. This voting principle underlies most of the electoral processes in those African countries where societies are divided into rival factions and common origins remain the most solid base for the formation of political loyalty. In such cases, voters join rival electoral blocs. If a leader enjoys the support of a large and loyal bloc of voters – his fellow tribesmen, the quality of his leadership as a factor for re-election largely loses its significance.

Undoubtedly, a multi-ethnic society may also function normally: problems arise when tribal affiliation generates loyalty that surpasses the allegiance to the nation as a whole. In African societies, a tribal identity usually prevails over the national one. Inter-tribal contradictions give rise to problems that are inevitably aggravated during the elections. However, the sense of national identity does not emerge by itself: the political leader must take care of its formation. Perhaps only one African leader succeeded in solving this problem – Tanzanian President Julius Nyerere. He carried out inefficient economic reforms but proved to be a political giant in terms of nation-building. Nyerere made sure that the people of his country considered and called themselves Tanzanians, and were proud of it.

On the other hand, first Kenyan President Jomo Kenyatta pursued an effective economic policy, but in the sphere of inter-tribal relations he could not and did not want to overcome contradictions, using the "divide and rule strategy" to consolidate his power. His ethnic group Kikuyu was receiving a disproportionately large share of public resources, while politicians – representatives of other peoples of the country – were subjected to severe repression. Neither Kenyatta nor his successor Daniel arap Moi sought to form a united nation, but rather focused on protecting interests of their fellow tribesmen.

The differences in the post-colonial political strategies of Tanzania and Kenya seem particularly clear: in the first case, it was the formation of a sense of national identity, while in the second – the exacerbation of inter-tribal rivalry.

The negative features of electoral process in African countries include the nomination of persons with criminal convictions as candidates for election. One would expect that such past would deprive them of their right to participate in an election or, at least, would not bring them victory. However, the constituency, as a rule, does not possess sufficient information to separate suspicions and rumours from reality. Voters receive unverified information, and they believe what they hear. A tribal bloc supports its politicians even if they are criminals. An elective office is attractive to those who deliberately focus on crime partly because such leaders gain the greatest benefits from staying in top government positions. It is not surprising, therefore, that former warlords, rebel leaders with criminal past (robberies, violence against the local population, arms and drug smuggling, etc.), and embezzlers often become heads of state. Among them were: Charles Taylor, former leader of the rebel National Patriotic Front of Liberia, who in 1997 became president of the country, and who in 2012 was accused of crimes against humanity by the International Criminal Court (ICC); Foday Sankoh, the former leader of the rebel group Revolutionary United Front of Sierra Leone, whose militants cut off hands of children and adults, raped women, and gained from the sale of "blood diamonds", and who became vice-president of Sierra Leone in 1997; Uhuru Kenyatta, who came to Kenya's highest public office in 2013 despite having being accused by the ICC of crimes against humanity in connection to the 2007 inter-tribal clashes; and so on.

There are many reasons that motivate leaders to try to become a "good" ruler. At least, they could leave the legacy of successful reforms, of which descendants would be proud. But not every leader knows how to achieve that. The qualification one obtains after several years of rule mainly limits itself to the ability to shuffle supporters like a card deck, to shift people within the patronage system, and to neutralise opponents, i.e., to manipulate and manoeuvre. However, the policy of reform is also fraught with danger, since the entourage of sycophants may oppose it, organise a palace revolution, and justify it to the outside world as necessary for "positive change".

Indeed, there are other winning strategies besides becoming a good ruler. For example, electoral fraud. Since a significant part of the population of Tropical Africa is illiterate and poorly informed, there is always an opportunity to explain to them the positive aspects of preserving the incumbent president in power despite his policy failures. There is an effective way to explain economic or political failures of a leader: to shift all the blame onto certain groups of the population, as Zimbabwean President R. Mugabe did when he blamed the "white farmers" for the country's economic failures and urged the citizens to restore historical justice, i.e., seize the lands of the white settlers.

You can win an election by bribing the electorate, especially since the incumbent president usually has more resources at his disposal than the opposition. Voter bribery can be carried out in two ways: wholesale and individually. The latter is expensive and complex and is aimed at certain political players capable of supporting the candidate during the election campaign and of mobilising large groups of the electorate. This was how Daniel arap Moi (Kenya) won the 1992 elections, having obtained the majority of votes.

Perhaps, the available resources do not allow the president to bribe all the necessary key figures individually. Then one can resort to "wholesale bribery", i.e., pay for a block of votes. Block voting is used mainly in rural communities, where everyone follows the advice of the chief. As a rule, the vote count demonstrates that 100% of all votes have been given to one candidate. Often politicians give empty promises and after the election they just sit in the office, but their supporters expect a new allocation of patronage funds before the next election.

However, bribery is also not a guarantee of success. A special experiment was conducted in the Republic of São Tomé and Príncipe. A group of neutral experts tried to track voter bribery during the first free multi-party elections in 1991. In some areas it was tracked, in others – it was not. Moreover, it turned out that some candidates who bribed in certain voting districts received most of their votes from other districts. Thus, it is desirable that this method of mobilising electorate be combined with real support of the local population.

Another way is to remove the strongest opponent from participation in the election. One can, for example, accuse him of corruption, especially since this is almost certainly true. At the same time, the leader-accuser demonstrates his own "firmness" in the fight against this vicious phenomenon. However, President O. Obasanjo, who rebuked Nigerian military leaders for corruption and became famous for his struggle against it in 1995, fell victim to his own revelations: he was charged with high treason and, in 2008, with embezzlement of $2.2 billion received under contracts for energy development[7].

There is also a factor of citizenship. Given the large tribal diversity of African countries and large-scale migrations, it is easy to identify "foreign" ancestors of the unwanted candidate and deprive him of the right to participate in elections. For instance, the incumbent president of Côte d'Ivoire, Alassane Ouattara, was not allowed to participate in the 2000 presidential election because his mother was from Burkina Faso. The constitution of the country states that a presidential candidate must have both parents Ivorian by birth, not by naturalisation. That is, people born in mixed marriages were excluded from the struggle for presidency. It should be noted that between one third and one half of the population of Ivory Coast are immigrants in the first, second, or third generations. Ouattara's rivals also pointed to his non-Ivorian origins during the 2010 elections, when he became president of the country (*de facto* since 11 April 2011) amidst an acute political crisis and with the support of UN peacekeepers[8].

Finally, it is possible to assassinate the competitor, as happened in Guinea-Bissau in 2009, when first the incumbent president João Bernardo Vieira was killed and then independent presidential candidate Bakiro Dabo, a member of the ruling African Party for the Independence of Guinea and Cape Verde, followed suit.

A fraudulent count of votes is another option. This strategy can be combined with other methods of struggle, for example, armed clashes between supporters of different candidates. This is what happened in 2006 in the DRC between supporters of President Joseph Kabila and vice-president Jean-Pierre Bemba. The clashes began with the announcement of the results of the first round of the presidential election, in which 45% of the participants voted for Kabila, while 20% supported Bemba. The fighting broke out on the eve of the second round[9].

---

[7] Orji N. Responses to Election Outcomes: The Aftermath of 2007 Elections in Nigeria and Kenya. *African and Asian Studies,* 2010, vol. 9, p. 433.

[8] Sadovskaya L.M. Pridet li mir v Kot-d'Ivuar? [Will There be Peace in Côte d'Ivoire?]. *Asia and Africa today,* 2012, vol. 6, pp. 31-37; vol. 7, pp. 49-53.

[9] http://www.newsru.com/world/22aug2006/kabila.html

Often voters understand that the incumbent president intends to win by any means and the way they vote is of little importance. In this case, they are less inclined to risk by voting for the opposition and fighting for their candidate.

A falsification of voting results can be kept in reserve until the very last moment, until it becomes clear that the balance is not in favour of the incumbent leader. For example, during the 2007 elections in Kenya, when the results of voting in districts were announced, the opposition decided that it was winning. Then suddenly it turned out that the president won with a narrow margin. However, it was not the margin but the blatancy of fraud that raised doubt: in one of the districts the number of votes went from 50,145 in the preliminary announcement to 75,261 in the final one[10].

The question arises: if it is possible to win unfairly with ease, why adhere to the democratic principles of accountability, transparency, etc.? Perhaps, that is why very few people adhere to them.

The aforementioned methods of achieving victory in elections prevail over the aspiration of an African ruler to win as a result of good governance. Most likely, this happens because if a leader wishes to keep his position by all means, he willingly sacrifices this strategy for the sake of more reliable and effective illegal methods. Moreover, Africa offers examples when it was impossible for a good leader to occupy the position he rightfully deserves. In this respect, the case of the re-election of Nigeria's Minister of the Federal Capital Territory of Abuja Nasir el-Rufai is interesting. Nigerians highly appreciated his work: in 2006 he won the prestigious Silverbird Man-of-the-Year Award. Having graduated with distinction from Harvard Business School, he showed himself to be a competent and enterprising politician and administrator and, using the advantages of his office, conducted an honest election campaign for a governor's post, but was not even nominated by his own party, presumably because of his tendency to make decisions independently.

Developed countries, which engaged in promoting democracy in Africa, sought to make African societies look like Western democracies, forgetting the path they had taken before they became what they were. The West did not achieve democracy in one go, and it would be unjust to expect this from developing societies. The changes taking place in Africa, which look like "the onset of an era of democracy", are more indicative of a statistical increase in the number of elections held on the continent than of the democratisation of political life. Meanwhile, the role of electoral processes should not be under-

---

[10] http://rusemp.ru/index.php/kenia3/3888-keniya-vybory-2007.html

estimated: in individual cases and to some extent, they can be viewed as "timid steps" along the path of democratisation.

The prospects for democratisation in the countries of Tropical Africa vary highly and are viewed in a broad political spectrum from Afro-pessimism to Afro-optimism. The political and economic situation in most of the countries of the continent does not facilitate either implementing serious democratic reforms or conducting free and fair presidential elections. The society is not yet ready to appreciate fully the ideas of democracy, and the state is not able (and often does not seek) to carry out effective political reforms.

Thus, the expectations of the democratisation that allegedly began in Africa at the end of the 20th century have proved unfounded for objective and subjective reasons. At the same time, certain political changes (holding elections and changing regimes as a result of electoral processes) indicate that democratic transformations on the continent are possible, albeit in a very distant future.

Ruslan Dmitriev
Ivan Zakharov

INTER-COMMUNAL CONFLICT IN NIGERIA AS A RESULT OF RELIGIOUS POLARISATION OF THE AFRICAN POPULATION[1]

The contemporary Africa has its own unique "face" in terms of its religious landscape. What is happening to the religions on the Black continent may become the model of confessional and civilization spatial development in the modern post-secular era[2].

Uneven demographic development of regions in the 20th–early 21st centuries led to major shifts in the distribution of believers – mostly Christian and Muslim – between the Global North and Global South. As a result, the share of believers in developing countries rose for all the world religions. Whereas in 1910, the Global North (developed countries of Europe, North America, Russia, Japan, Australia, and New Zealand) composed over 82% of world's Christians, a mere century later the figure dropped to 39%. Meanwhile, the Global South (developing countries of Africa, Latin America, Asia and Oceania) saw an increase in its share of the Christian population from 18 to 61%, i.e. almost 3.5 times! The shift of the global religious landscape to the South resulted in an increase of Africa's share in *all the world's religions.*

Currently, Africa is home to over 540 million Christians (the third place among macro-regions, or 23.5% of the Global Christian population)[3]and 420 million Muslims (the second place in the world, or about 27% of the global Muslim population)[4]. Whereas it comes and will come second to Asia in share of Muslim population, by 2020 the African continent will obtain the

---

[1] First published in *The Bulletin of Irkutsk State University. Series «Political Science and Religion Studies».* Issue 13, 2015.

[2] Gorokhov S.A., Khristov T.T. *Religii narodov mira* [Religions of the Peoples of the World]. Moscow, KNORUS, 2010. 422 p.

[3] Johnson T.M., Zurlo G.A., Hickman A.W., Crossing P.F. Christianity 2015: Religious Diversity and Personal Contact. *International Bulletin of Missionary Research*, 2015, vol. 39, no. 1, pp. 28-29.

[4] Johnson T.M., Ross K. R., eds. *Atlas of Global Christianity.* Edinburgh, Edinburgh University Press Ltd, 2009. 364 p.

largest Christian population of 630 million, outrunning Latin America and Europe[5].

In the early 20th century, no African state ranked among the top ten countries with the highest Christian population. A century later the situation has changed dramatically, with Nigeria and DR Congo joining the rank of the largest Christian countries and Ethiopia projected to join them by 2050. In 1910, only Egypt and Morocco were among the top ten largest Muslim population countries; however, in 2010, Nigeria and Algeria followed suit[6].

Among the reasons for the ever-increasing African share in the world religions are a high birth rate, and effective missionary work conducted by members of religious groups (first and foremost, Christianity).

The total fertility rate (average number of children that would be born to a woman over her lifetime) in the period 2010–2015 was 3.0 in Northern Africa and 5.1 in Sub-Saharan Africa[7]. The birth-rate delivers 96% of the region's Muslim population growth on the continent, which is much higher in comparison to African population growth rates in general. Thus, the total fertility rate of Muslims in the Sub-Saharan Africa constitutes 5.5, which is 0.9 greater than that of non-Muslims (4.6)[8]. Consequently, conversion influences the growth of the Christian community to a far greater degree than the Muslim one, delivering nearly 29% of the Cristian population's annual growth. What testifies to the efficiency of Christians missionary work is that in 2010 Africa saw over 3.3 million people converted to Christianity, which delivers over 15 per cent pf the total growth of the Christian community in Africa. Regarding the missionary activities, Nigeria, DR Congo, Ethiopia, Tanzania, and Kenya come first, with 200–500 thousand converts to Christianity throughout 2010[9].

Therefore, because of the wide influence not only of Christianity and Islam but also syncretic beliefs and a high level of ethnic diversity of the population, the confessional situation in Africa is extraordinarily complicated. The

---

[5]*Christianity in its Global Context, 1970–2020. Society, Religion, and Mission.* South Hamilton, Center for the Study of Global Christianity, 2013. 92 p.

[6] Ibid.

[7]*World Population Prospects: The 2012 Revision.* Available at: http://esa.un.org/ unpd/wpp/index.htm (accessed 13.04.2015).

[8]*The Future of the Global Muslim Population.* Available at: http://www.pewforum.org/2011/01/27/the-future-of-the-global-muslim-population/ (accessed 14.02.2015).

[9] Johnson T.M., Ross K. R., eds. *Atlas of Global Christianity.* Edinburgh, Edinburgh University Press Ltd, 2009. 364 p.

competition of major religions always existed in Africa and is still important: moreover "palm of victory" has shifted from one religion to another frequently enough. Thus, in 1910, traditional beliefs came first in Africa (58.0%), by the third part of the 20th century they gave way to Islam (about 38%), but the dawn of a new century ushered in a Christian lead (46%) on the continent (this trend is projected to remain at least up to 2050).

The religious landscape of the contemporary Africa blends high diversity[10] and deep religiosity of the local population. According to Gallup International/WIN research[11], Africa has the most religious population in the world. Such countries as Ghana, Nigeria, Kenya, Cameroon and South Sudan rank among the top 10 religious countries (over 75% of population are extremely religious). The African Christian churches stand out against churches in America and Europe with traditional attitudes and moralisation.. Thus, for instance, Anglican bishops in Africa refuse to ordain homosexual bishops, persisting on traditional interpretation of the Bible. These features indicate establishment of an African-type Christianity that is different from that of the West. However, Muslim communities nurture their traditional heritage across the continent to almost the same extent.

The African religious landscape has its regional varietiations. Northern Africa is an Islam-dominant region whereas Sub-Saharan Africa is much more religiously diverse, with a Christian majority in the most countries. Thus, by the early 21st century, owing to the rapid expansion of Christianity and Islam, the continent was split into almost equal parts between Christian and Islam beliefs. The religious and cultural landscape's border goes through the Sahel Zone, dividing the Islam-dominant North and the Christian-dominant South.

To some extent, the complexity of religious composition of the Sahel Zone factors into the political fragility of this particular part of Africa, which became a development base for some international terrorist groups. The well-known Russian Africanists A. Vasilyev and A. Potapov believe that "ethnic and/or religious beliefs and clichés – either new or old, socio-ethnic and religious psychology – have become the main driving factors and triggers of the

---

[10] Gorokhov S.A. Religioznaja identichnost' kak faktor formirovanija konfessional'nyh regionov sovremennogo mira [Religious Identity as a Factor of Confessional Regions Formation in the Present-day World]. *Vestnik Moskovskogo Unviersiteta, Seriya Geografiya*, 2012, vol. 5, pp. 49-55.

[11] *Global index of religiosity and atheism – 2012. WIN-Gallup International.* Available at: http://blog.scona.com.ua/pictures/files/RED-C-Press-Release-Religion-and-Atheism-25-7-12.pdf (accessed 27.01.2015).

conflict evolution" [12]. As a result, the continent turns into "battlefield" for two world major religions – Christianity and Islam and this causes an extreme politicisation of religion in the region.

Nigeria, the most populated African country, being a home for 72 million Christians and roughly the same number of Muslims, represents an example of inter-communal contradictions and politicisation of religion (see Table 1). The country ranks 7th in the world and 1st in Africa for largest Christian and Muslim population. By 2050, the population of Nigeria is projected to have 139 million Christians and a similar number of Muslims and will rise to the 5th in the world on this indicator.

Table 1

Size of Major Religious Groups in Nigeria[13]

Religion	1910 г.		1970 г.		2010 г.	
	mln	%	mln	%	mln	%
Muslims	4.9	26.0	22.5	44.0	72.3	45.7
Christians	0.2	1.1	22.7	44.0	72.3	45.7
Traditional believers	13.7	73.0	6.0	12.0	13.1	8.3

However, there is no reliable data on the modern religious composition of the country. Thus, Census 2006 omitted the question about religious affiliation due to the fact that it was highly sensitive for the Nigerian society, which is divided over religion. According to the official data, Muslims and Christians constitute 50.5% and 48.2% of the Nigerian population respectively in 2003[14]. Nevertheless, the Christian community in the country has already outnumbered that of Germany and the Muslim population in Nigeria is larger than that of a traditionally Islamic country such as Egypt.

It took one generation to make Nigeria a predominantly Christian country. According to the 1952 Census 21.1% of the population practiced Christianity, 47.4% – Muslims, and 31.6% was adherents of other religions (mostly Tradi-

[12]*Strany Afriki 2002* [The countries of Africa 2002]. Moscow, Institute for African Studies RAS, 2002. 704 p.

[13] Johnson T.M., Ross K. R., eds. *Atlas of Global Christianity*. Edinburgh, Edinburgh University Press Ltd, 2009. 364 p.

[14] Lalasz R. *In the News: The Nigerian Census*. Available at: http://www.prb.org/ Articles/2006/IntheNewsTheNigerianCensus.aspx (accessed 18.04.2015).

tional believes)[15]. Half a century later, even according to official data the percentage of Christian population more than doubled and the share of the Muslim population remaining the same.

The size of the Christian population increased mostly by virtue of missionary work of evangelical churches, which compose almost half of Nigeria's Protestant population (26.5 mln). Among them are most notably the Pentecostal Churches, such as the Apostolic Mission Church of Nigeria, the Redeemed Christian Church, the Apostolic Church of Jesus Christ, the Mission of Evangelical Church, etc.

Presently, Nigeria is de facto split into two parts, with Islam-dominant North and Christianity-dominant South. Inter-communal relations in Nigeria have always been strained and the tension was increased in the late 1980's because of the influence of fundamentalist religious movements (mostly Islamic) across the globe. As a result, unresolved issues triggered public protests in Nigeria, which later escalated into religious conflicts – first and foremost between Muslims and Christians.

The constitution of Nigeria mandates that the state authorities have no right to consider any religion as a state religion, although there are no direct guidelines regarding whether Nigeria is secular or not[16]. However, in November 1999, Sharia Law was adopted as the public legal framework in Zamfara state, which was later followed by 11 more states in the North of Nigeria. The fact that 12 out of 36 Nigerian states introduced Sharia law a matter of concern to the Christian community, which was afraid of the entire country becoming an Islamic state, in which Christians would suffer discrimination.

"Boko Haram", a fundamentalist terrorist organization, is the core element of the Muslim-Christian inter-communal conflict in Nigeria. The mission of this group is stipulated in its full name, i.e. "*Jama'atu Ahlis Sunna Lidda'awati wal-Jihad*", which stands for "Community of the Followers who Spread the Teaching of Prophet and Jihad". With a headquarters in Maiduguri in the North-West of the country, it has been recruiting troops under the disguise of an educational centre which was attracting children from poor families – mostly from the largest ethnic group in this part of Nigeria – the Kanuri. Here the organisation got its name "Boko Haram" which is usually

---

[15] Ostien P. *Percentages by Religion of the 1952 and 1963 Populations of Nigeria's Present 36 States*. Available at: http://www3.qeh.ox.ac.uk/pdf/nrn/BP1Ostien.pdf (accessed 04.03.2015).

[16] Nigerija. Spravochno-monograficheskoe izdanie [Nigeria. Monographical Booklet]. Moscow, Institute for African Studies, 2013. 378 p.

translated as "Western education is Evil" [17]. The Muslim radical group's resentment over Western education is connected to the former prevalence of Christian missionaries in this field. Soon after establishment, "Boko Haram" masterminded virulent attacks against the Nigerian government, accusing them of favouring Christianisation by means of imposing "the Western bourgeois culture" on the population. Among the notorious terror acts by "Boko Haram" are so called "Christmas day bombings" committed in Christian churches in the central part of the country (2011), the attack on the City of Kano (2012), the kidnapping of over 270 Christian schoolgirls in Chibok in Borno state (2014) and the burning of 16 villages and towns in the Borno state (2015).

The "Boko Haram" activists managed to institute control over a considerable land area in the North-Eastern part of the country (the states of Borno, Yobe, Adamawa, Bauchi and Gombe) and expanded further to the neighbouring countries (Cameroon, Niger and Chad). In April 2015, Abubakar Shekau, the leader of "Boko Haram", swore his allegiance to the Islamic State (IS), the group was renamed "The Western African province of the Islamic State" [18], thereby it was plugged into the global terrorist network. The government of Nigeria, under the head of Goodluck Jonathan (a Christian from the South-East of Nigeria) made an attempt to initiate negotiations with Islamist, but due to total breakdown of peaceful means of conflict resolution it moved to the battleground in early 2014. The military confrontation between Islamists and the Nigerian military claimed the lives of thousands and turned over 3 million into displaced persons, including about 1 million over the last year[19, 20]. As the violence in Nigeria reached its climax, it raised con-

[17] Q&A: Islamic group spreading terror in Nigeria. Available at: http://edition.cnn.com/2012/01/02/world/africa/boko-haram-nigeria/index.html?_s=PM:AFRICA (accessed 24.01.2015).

[18] The leader of "Boko Haram" swore its allegiance to the Islamic state. *Lenta.ru*, 08.03.2015. Available at: http://lenta.ru/news/2015/03/08/haram/ (accessed 17.03.2015).

[19] The President of Nigeria Muhammad Buhari. *Echo Moskvy. 48 minutes*, 08.04.2015. Available at: http://echo.msk.ru/programs/48minut/1525994-echo/ (accessed 15.04.2015).

[20] Boko Haram May Have Displaced Over a Million in Nigeria. Available at: http://www.iom.int/cms/en/sites/iom/home/news-and-views/press-briefing-notes/pbn-2015/pbn-listing/boko-haram-may-have-displaced-ov.html (accessed 03.03.2015).

cern at the International criminal court, with a prosecutor coming up with respective statements late 2014[21].

In prospect the escalation of Islam-Christianity conflict may split the country into the Christian South and the Muslim North echoing the scenario of Sudan in 2011 when Christian-dominant South Sudan proclaimed independence.

In March 2015, Nigeria saw presidential elections which brought to presidency Muhammad Buhari (an adherent of Islam). He ran away with the elections going ahead of his main rival – then incumbent president Goodluck Jonathan – with a margin of 2.7 million. As the elections showed, the Nigerian society is still divided by religious allegiance: Islam-dominant North ensured the victory of M. Buhari whereas G. Jonathan led the poles in the Christian South-East of the country[22]. The main reason for M. Buhari's victory was that he pursued order in the North of Nigeria, urging reconciliation with his motto "My ambition is not worth the blood of Nigerians" [23]. Known as a true believer, this Muslim president is probably destined to be the most acceptable partner in talks with Muslim fundamentalists. We cherish the hope that M. Buhari will set Nigeria free from terrorism and put aside cultural and religious contradictions within the society.

The success of the new federal administration of Nigeria could prove that future Africa may become not just a battleground for stiff inter-confessional confrontation, but also a bridge for a dialogue between different denominations.

---

[21] ICC lawyer, activist accuse Nigeria presidential candidate of inciting violence. *Jurist*, 23.01.2015. Available at: http://jurist.org/paperchase/2015/01/icc-lawyer-activist-accuse-nigerian-presidential-candidate-of-inciting-violence.php (accessed 02.02.2015).

[22] The Incumbent Nigerian President lost Election for the First Time. *Novaya Gazeta*, 01.04.2015. Available at: http://www.novayagazeta.ru/news/1692817.html (accessed 15.04.2015).

[23] The President of Nigeria Muhammad Buhari. *Echo Moskvy. 48 minutes*, 08.04.2015. Available at: http://echo.msk.ru/programs/48minut/1525994-echo/ (accessed 15.04.2015).

Leonid Fituni
Irina Abramova

ARESERVE ARMY OF ISIS: RESOURCES AND MANOEUVRE[1]

In the past few years the struggle against Islamic terrorism seems to have boiled down to fighting the Islamic State of Iraq and Syria (ISIS), also known as the Islamic State (IS). The second decade of the 21st century saw the ISIS encroachment into vast territories of Asia and North Africa[2]. ISIS has been successfully retaining its control over these territories in spite of the effort taken by a military coalition of over 60 states[3]. In this regard, the question arises: what resources enable ISIS – this ill-equipped, inadequately trained and underfunded enemy, which is also noted for mediaeval atrocities, – to persevere in resistance?

Simple as it is, the answer to this question involves uncomfortable realities. Far from political correctness, this answer fits neither the perspective of the so called "civilized world" nor the clichés of democratic discourse.

In the language of the British political economist D. Ricardo, the answer is as follows: the "market supply" of IS/ISIS is currently meeting a certain "market demand" among the elites and vast popular masses in the East and the West alike. High in the Middle East, this demand is also tangible in the West, and not just in the Muslim community.

A popular belief held in Russia and almost everywhere else (but not by everyone, to our regret) is that IS/ISIS phenomenon is to be nipped in the bud as it poses a threat to the very physical existence and civilizational development of many nations.

A further look at IS/ISIS phenomenon brings to the table three main questions. First, where do the funds come from and what are the limits to the group's influence? The answer to this question would reveal the true scope of the IS/ISIS terrorist threat. Second, what is the spillover effect of the "IS/ISIS

---

[1] First published in *Asia and Africa Today*. Issue 12, 2016.

[2] Fituni L.L. Agressivnye negosudarstvennye aktory – novaja ugroza razvitiju Afriki [Aggressive Non-State Actors – a New Threat to Africa's Development]. *Journal of the Institute for African Studies*, 2015, no. 1, pp. 14-20.

[3] Remarks by General John Allen, then Special Presidential Envoy for the Global Coalition to Counter ISIL. Doha, Qatar, 03.06.2015. Available at: https://www.brookings.edu/wp-content/uploads/2015/04/060315BROOKING SDO-HA.pdf

project" on adjacent regions exposed to its direct and "indirect influence", i.e. Africa and the Middle East? Last but not least, how great an influence does ISIS exert on Western societies, including Europe, Russia (our primary concern) and neighbouring CIS countries?

"EAST IS EAST, AND WEST IS WEST"

ISIS inside and "European Jihadism" outside the Arab world are considered to be negative side-effects derived from the growing political self-consciousness, self-esteem and self-identity among Muslims in Arab and European countries respectively. The "Arab spring" gave new impetus to the these *"self's"*[4]. Just like blissfully ignorant characters of a European movie, the "Arab Spring" let the genie out of the bottle into the complex modern world dominated by IT gurus and political pundits. Shut up for centuries inside the vase and constrained by Muslim societies with long-lived customs and taboos, the genie of destruction is now free to go.

These destructive forces unleashed by the "Arab Spring" shattered fragile secular structures of Arab societies, plunged these societies into political chaos and civil conflicts, and destroyed economies that were already weak. This further aggravated social problems and pushed people towards impulsive actions and wrong decisions, religious radicalism being one of them. In some areas large-scale Muslim radicalisation got the upper hand as the moderate Muslim leaders failed to live up to (de-facto groundless) hopes for the solution of social and economic problems caused by the collapse of authoritarian and corrupt Arab regimes.

As revolutionary unrest sent shivers across the entire Muslim word, the pace of radicalisation varied between countries. This fact is indirectly substantiated by the research of sociological think tanks, including Pew Research Center. We can see that the level of support for ISIS among Muslims in Africa and the Middle East, while being very high in some countries, is much lower in others (see Figure 1).

Ideologically and economically, those who share ISIS ideas and regard ISIS actions as a natural "response to the persecution of Muslims" seem to be the IS/ISIS 'strategic reserve'. It is where troops are recruited, funds and donations are raised. And it is where IS/ISIS get logistical support while estab-

---

[4] Fituni L.L., Abramova I.O. Negosudarstvennye i kvazigosudarstvennye aktory Bol'shogo Blizhnego Vostoka i problema «evrodzhihadizma» [Non- and Quasi-State Actors of the Great Middle East and the Phenomenon of Eurojihadism]. *Asia and Africa Today*, 2015, no. 11, pp. 2-11.

lishing arms trafficking and human trafficking channels, dealing with paperwork and temporary shelter to name a few.

The East's wants are contradictory. Seeking to benefit from European well-being here and now, a majority of people in the East, however, are reluctant to incur "costs" which are deemed intrinsic in liberal and democratic societies but which are counted as injustice, vulgarity, promiscuity, and perversions in traditional ones. These conflicting desires generate cognitive dissonance not only in the whole of society but even within entire civilizational areas. It is this dissonance that accounts for the failure of most "colour revolutions" and "Arab Springs" as well as further grave repercussions.

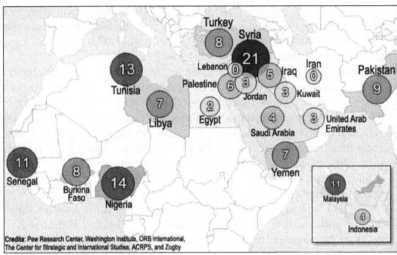

Figure 1. Potential ISIS Reserve in some countries of Africa, Middle East and Asia (% of the population which shares the ISIS ideas, results of the opinion poll 2014/2015)[5].
Footnote: "0" stands for less than 1 percent.

The IS/ISIS phenomenon in its current form of terrorist group/caliphate is nothing but a radical manifestation of this cognitive dissonance, implanted by politicians and pundits not only in the Eastern societies of Iraq, Syria, Egypt, Libya, Nigeria, Afghanistan, Somalia, but also in the Muslim societies of Europe, America and Asia-Pacific.

---

[5] http://metrocosm.com/support-isis-muslim-world-perceptions-vs-reality/

Although it is commonly acknowledged even in the West that ISIS was bred by the second American war against Saddam Hussein in Iraq, the nature of ISIS should not to be defined as exclusively a Middle Eastern issue or an outcome of Washington's geopolitical regional project.

As more countries engaged in the anti-terrorist operations in Syria and Iraq, ISIS claimed responsibility for an increasing number of terror attacks in Europe. The IS/ISIS expansion triggered an acute migration crisis in Europe, which further exacerbated latent social tensions within the European community. As many politicians and researchers put it, the crisis cast doubt on whether it would be possible to keep the EU as it is now.

It is hard to say whether it was the original plan, but IS/ISIS factor is not just a terrorist threat any longer. As a hard, social engineering tool, it appeals to both groups of the European political establishment – those who seek to "dilute" national identity in countries which historically came to exist as nation-states (compared to settler colonial countries) and those who resist any (including natural) ethnic and civilizational transformation of "nations".

If you take the statement mentioned above at face value and assume that the process is under control, it will then become clear why some European leaders continue to support migration from other civilizations, whereas others ignite nationalistic sentiment which borders xenophobia. To put it in another way, the "IS/ISIS phenomenon" has turned out to be an instrument of global governance.

HUMAN RESOURCES OF THE "RESERVE ARMY"

ISIS considers all Muslims in the EU (be it those who settled down or newcomers) as its strategic reserve in Europe, no matter what their political preferences are. It has devised and is implementing active and passive recruitment strategy/tactics for the Caliphate. By employing both traditional recruitment channels (mosque, sermons, religious clubs, and circulated press) and modern ones (IT, social networks, charities and educational bodies, NGOs, cultural communities, labour unions and associations to name a few), ISIS aims at setting up a multi-million community capable of influencing EU politics and public sentiment.

Estimates of the Muslim population in the EU depend on what methods are used and how you define a Muslim. Politics and ideology, along with political correctness and reluctance to become a *bête noir*, have their own bearing on the final figures published in the press. Official and semi-official data from the EU and national sources say that Muslims comprise 15–20 million out of the half a billion population of Western and Central Europe

(28 EU member-states plus Norway and Switzerland). Yet Muslim organizations claim that the Muslim population in Europe is as big as 25 million.

As our field research has shown, Muslim organizations in Europe proceed from the size of the mosque community. It is true that, with few exceptions, nobody asks for citizenship documents or a residence card in the mosque. At the same time heads of communities and grassroots alike may be fully aware that a person on the pray mat next to them has no such documents. In other words, based on the actual attendance and not adjusted for political or legal purposes, estimates of the Muslim population based on mosque sources will inevitably be bigger than those from official governmental sources. One should, of course, also bear in mind that in some European countries, the larger the community is, the larger is the size of financial support it can get from the government[6].

Before the 2015–2016 migration crisis, it was commonly believed that by 2030 Muslims would make up 10 percent of the EU population. This forecast was later adjusted by the man-made migration crisis of 2015–2016. There is no shadow of doubt that the forecast figures will go up for all EU member-states. According to IS/ISIS propaganda sources dated 2014–2015, spiritual leaders claimed that soon enough one in five Europeans (it is not clear whether they were talking about the EU or the whole of Europe) will preach Islam.

In terms of absolute number of Muslims, Russia tops the rank in the European continent. The estimate is that the Muslim population, by and large local, falls within a range from 17 to 21.5 million (i.e. 12–15 per cent of the total Russian population). The number of Russian Muslims is growing far more sharply than that of other confessions, which is partly a result of the Muslim immigration from Central Asia and Azerbaijan. The inflow of immigrants may decline by 2030 but is unlikely to come to a halt.

Regarding the Muslim population in the EU, Belgium and France come first and enjoy the largest share of Muslim citizens (citizens, not residents!) compared to other EU countries, which is between 6 and 8 percent according to conservative estimates and taking into account only naturalised migrants. These countries are followed by Denmark, Great Britain, Sweden, Germany, the Netherlands, Austria (4–5 percent). Switzerland, non-EU member, belongs to the same group.

---

[6] Abramova I.O., Fituni L.L. *Arhiv polevyh issledovanij. 2008–2016. Dos'e 8–24* [Archives of Field Studies. 2008–2016. Archive files 8-24].

In Spain, Italy and non-EU Norway, Muslims contribute to a much lower but still substantial part of the population (between 2 and 3 percent).

The number of followers of Islam is growing at an increasing pace in Sweden, Belgium, Austria, Great Britain, Norway, France and Italy, with most Central Europe countries accommodating insignificant Muslim communities (0.3% or even less). Given the current immigration level and the high birth rate, even according to official estimates the Muslim population in Europe will exceed 30 million by 2030 (without the Balkan states that will possibly join the EU). The number of Muslim residents living in the EU on a permanent basis is at least twice as large as that of EU Muslim citizens.

RESOURCE MANOEUVRING

How successful is ISIS in manoeuvring its "reserve army" and exploiting its resources?

The most straightforward way is to call up the "army reserve" for IS/ISIS service in the Middle East, and to use "sleeper cells" or "lone wolves" to commit a terrorist act outside the Middle East, first of all in Europe.

As the research has revealed, economic factors are not decisive while exploiting human resources of the "reserve army". People do not necessarily have to languish in poverty to be easily recruited as ISIS mercenaries. Statistics shows that the number of recruited mercenaries correlates with the national GDP per capita and Human Development Index (HDI). A hefty part of ISIS mercenaries come from developed economies with low inequality and developed political institutions.

Among other factors of ISIS recruitment are the size of the Muslim population in the country and its ethnic cohesion. Most ISIS troops from the EU are recruited in countries that are more coherent in terms of ethnicity and language and where immigrants find it difficult to assimilate. This shows that the reasons for fighters' inflow to ISIS from abroad is determined not so much by economy and politics, but by the mindset and hurdles to assimilate in Western countries, as can be seen from Table 1.

Regarding the ISIS "reserve army", it is necessary to acknowledge that many fighters come from former USSR republics, including Russia. This year Gulmorod Halimov, also known as al-Tajiki, succeeded as the head of the group after Tarhan Batirashvili, also known as Abu-Umar Ash-Shishani had been killed in an antiterrorist operation[7]. Born in Georgia and also known

---

[7] Laymen may wrongly get the impression that numerous al-Shishani come from a family of prominent military officers. In fact, the word "ash-Shishani" stands for

as Umar the Chechen, Tarkhan Batirashvilli (father – Christian Georgian, mother – Chechen) was liquidated in an airstrike, 4 March, in the Syrian city of Al-Shaddadah, as reported by the Pentagon. Another source claims that he was killed in July in the battle near the Iraqi town of ash-Shirkat. Gulmuldon Halimov, a former leader of the Tajiki riot squad, also seems to have been in the ISIS reserve for a while before coming to the forefront last April. Charged with treason and becoming a wanted person in Tajikistan, he was also put on a US sanction list last year[8].

"The reserve army" on the ISIS periphery, i.e. Europe, the Caucasus, Central Asia, and some African countries takes the form of "sleeper cells" or "lone wolves". The latter are those members of the "reserve army" that are not actively involved in, affiliated with or represented by a particular group or network with a name and structure. A "sleeper cell" is an independent radical group that has certain plans but takes no action until the signal from above comes.

ISIS, for instance, is known to have set up a "sleeper cell" to plan and commit terrorist acts in the future, which was also mentioned by Abdelhak Khiam, the head of Moroccan Central Bureau of Judicial Investigation (BCIJ)[9]. He noted that IS strategy in Morocco has been radically transformed. Those who share Islamist ideology or ISIS ideas have been instructed to stay in Morocco and breed "sleeper cells" for large-scale operations. He illustrated these statement referring to an operation where a Chad citizen (ISIS supporter who was planning a number of terrorist attacks in Moroccan cities, including Rabat), was arrested in Tangier. Among the plans were "large-scale attacks on Western diplomatic buildings and tourist attractions". The terrorist was supposed to target the embassy of a foreign country in Rabat, a hotel, a casino and a foreign cultural centre in Tangier[10].

Table 1

"Chechen" in Arabic and is part of the nickname which refers to the country of origin (ethnicity) of the fighter.

[8] http://ecrats.org/ru/situation/status/6263

[9] BCIJ came to exist in 2015 to fight against crime and the terrorist threat. It is subordinate to General Directorate for Territorial Surveillance – a key intelligence body in the country.

[10] http://tass.ru/mezhdunarodnaya-panorama/3313668

ISIS fighters as a % of Muslim population[11, 12]

Country	Muslim population, thousands	ISIS fighters	Fighters/Population, %
Finland	42	70	0.1667
Belgium	638	470	0.0737
Ireland	43	30	0.0698
Sweden	451	300	0.0665
Austria	475	300	0.0632
Tunisia	10,349	6,050	0.0580
Norway	144	81	0.0563
Germany	1,770	800	0.0451
UK	2,800	780	0.0279
France	4,155	990	0.0241
Russia	21,513	2,180	0.0102
Turkmenistan	4,407	380	0.086
Tajikistan	6,805	390	0.0057
Kazakhstan	7,131	300	0.0042
Azerbaijan	7,584	220	0.0028
Uzbekistan	23,898	500	0.0021
Kyrgyzstan	4,117	500	0.0012
Egypt	80,024	600	0.0007
Algeria	34,780	170	0.0005
Indonesia	204,847	700	0.0003

In 2016, mass media reported that "sleeper cells" masterminded and orchestrated huge terror attacks in Brussels and Paris. "Sleeper cells" also committed infamous terror attacks in the south and west of France as well as Germany. It is true, however, that ISIS has recently got into the habit of claiming responsibility for almost all the massive terror attacks, labeling

---

[11] The figures for Russia may have a very high margin of error since they often include any Russian speakers, i.e. immigrants from former Soviet Republics and/or so-called Muslim "refugees" who migrated to Turkey, UAE, Qatar, and the EU states through various quotas and programmes in the post-Soviet years. These people are not currently the citizens of the Russian Federation.

[12] http://metrocosm.com/foreign-isis-fighters/

them as "ISIS operations", especially when a suspect or a culprit comes from an Arab country or is an immigrant of Arab origin, or even just a Muslim.

Yerlan Katin, Director of Kazakhstan Institute for Strategic Studies, does not consider the group responsible for the terror attack in Aktobe[13], 2016, to be directly related to any international organisation. As he put it, "The statement by the MFA head has been widely misinterpreted by those who claim that the Aktobe group is an ISIS cell in Kazahstan. This is not true. What is more, the financial statement did not refer to the group affiliation of Aktobe terrorists. I, personally, believe that the Aktobe terrorist group is not subordinate to any international terrorist organisation"[14].

Then, however, the author contradicts himself, claiming that experts label the groups similar to the one in Aktobe as "sleeper cells". These "sleeper cells" are occasionally supplied with propaganda materials, particularly by IS/ISIS.

IS/ISIS is known for its active propaganda, uploading posts, video and audio files in the social networks. During only 2013–2016 5 so called official ISIS videos were distributed in which members from Kazakhstan call for attacks. One can also find in social networks dozens and hundreds of photos/videos by fighters from Central Asia, as well as their numerous accounts. Two weeks before the Aktobe attack an audio message went viral in the social networks, calling on fighters to carry out attacks in Kazakhstan and other countries.

Y. Karin underlined that, five days before the Aktobe attack the US State Department announced a risk of terror attacks in Europe, which indicates the build-up of a terrorist threat. In any case, he claims, the terror threat comes from "sleeper cells" and "long wolves", which makes it difficult to prevent these attacks[15].

---

[13] 5 June 2016 the city of Aktobe (former Aktyubinsk) in Kazakhstan witnesses a terrorist attack on the military base and 2 gun shops, some 5 people killed and about 40 injured. The authorities of Kazakhstan tend to believe that the responsibility is on takfirists, who may not relate directly to ISIS. The ISIS propagandists, however, attribute the terror attack to the caliphate fighters, referring to Abu Muhammad al-Adnani, emir of "Vilayat Sinai", who sent a new propaganda message shortly before the attack, urging supporters across the globe (not just in Aktobe or Kazakhstan) to carry out violent attacks on the eve of the holy month of Ramadan, which sent a signal to "sleeper cells" and "lone wolves".

[14] http://www.zakon.kz/4799985-e.karin.html
[15] Ibid.

Both Russian senior officials and anti-terror security experts repeatedly express their concern regarding the spread of ISIS ideas among Russian and other CIS citizens. For the number of our compatriots that joined terrorist groups and left Russia to join ISIS, see the table. It is not only about cannon fodder, i.e. those who join the army, but also about those who seek to plug into ISIS strategic human resources. The latter fall into three main groups: candidates for prestigious/lucrative jobs within ISIS (high-skilled experts, including doctors, engineers, chemists, IT-specialists); women and girls in the pursuit of Muslim happiness; unemployed, low-skilled people disoriented by propaganda, who are desperate to get job security, settle down in a family or join peaceful Muslim life – these dreams are a far cry from reality.

Numerous and socially significant, the ISIS "reserve army", however, is lacking in coherence and poorly consolidated. ISIS falls short of tapping into its potential, with many members are reluctant to follow instructions imposed from above and with intelligence services being on the lookout. This army is nevertheless subject to the scrutiny of radical Islamists and it may develop in unexpected ways.

* * *

The research shows that the ISIS reserve army in Europe will continue to exist for the foreseeable future. Just as ISIS inherited a lot of resources from "Al-Qaeda", the army may be later passed over to ISIS' successor. The role of other cultures and elements from another civilization, including the "reserve army", will be on the rise in European societies. Demographic and socio-political trends of the European society alike will contribute to such development. The "reserve army" can keep feeding on the ideas of radical Islam and breeding jihadist militants for a long time.

The military victory over IS/ISIS is unlikely to put a halt to the turbulence in the Middle East and on the CIS southern borders. Unsettled issues, seeds of violence and the ease of committing terror attacks will have long-term repercussions.

This, however, does not mean that Russia and its allies do not need to combine their might to create an extended anti-terrorist front, ideally including our geopolitical "friends/competitors" in the West. This front would reduce violence in the region and contain the pockets of IS/ISIS resistance.

\it should also be borne in mind that ISIS and terrorist threats in general (as well as a reproduced syndrome of "Eastern threat") are an instrument actively employed for consolidation and global governance. In this regard, should the IS/ISIS threat be exterminated, it cannot be ruled out that it will be replaced by another guided group in the "soft underbelly" of Russia, posing a threat to national security.

Valentina Gribanova

STUDENTS FROM THE COUNTRIES OF NORTH AFRICA IN THE RUSSIAN HIGHER SCHOOLS: PROBLEMS OF ADAPTATION[1]

One of the key objectives with the Russian education is to make it more competitive. The "Concept of long-term socio-economic development of the Russian Federation until 2020" adopted by the Russian government stipulates that it is a must to attract foreign students into Russia. The action plan is that by 2020 the share of foreign students will be at least 5%, with the revenue from them being at least 10% from the total education income. The designers of the concepts believe that such figures will prove high quality of the Russian education, promoting Russia as a leader in the export of education services.

The number of foreign students in Russia serves an indicator of Russia's integration into the global market and has a history of its own. Following Second World War, the Soviet Union accommodated students from Eastern Europe and Asia, with Africa, including Northern Africa, following suit. Over 40 years from 1950 to 1990, the number of foreign students in the Soviet Union rocketed 20 times, reaching 126.5 thousand, i.e. 10.8% of the total number of foreign students world-wide. Regarding the number of foreign students, the Soviet Union ranked third after the US and France[2].

The share of North African students in the Soviet Union in 1950–1986 constituted 12.5%[3]. It was due to the fact that the Soviet Union provided substantial economic and logistical support that the burgeoning independent Maghreb states were interested in Soviet education. The Soviet Union prepared 10 thousand experts for Egypt. It also contributed with Algeria, a focus being on education. Algerian students studied in about 22 Soviet colleges[4]. Although the Soviet Union did not see eye to eye with Western-oriented Morocco and Tunisia, over five thousand Moroccans got a degree in the Soviet

---

[1] First published in *Pedagogy*. Issue 7, 2016.

[2] World Educational Report. 1993. 378 p. P. 106.

[3] Arefiev A.L., Sheregi F.E. *Inostrannye studenty v rossijskih VUZah* [Foreign students in Russian Universities]. Moscow, TSSI, 2014. 228 p. P. 56.

[4] Zherlitsina N.A. Strategicheskoe partnerstvo Rossii i Alzhira v uslovijah krizisa: potencial i vyzovy [The strategic partnership between Russia and Algeria in a crisis: the potential and challenges]. *Vestnik universiteta*, 2015, no. 8, pp. 24-32. P. 26.

Union[5]. When it comes to Tunisia, over 1,500 experts are members of the Tunisia Association of Soviet Alumni[6].

With Russia on the way to the market economy, the profit issue came to the fore. Foreign students still opt for Russia since the Russian degree is still in high demand and the tuition fee is quite affordable. In 2012 Russia was accommodating 7,609 students from North Africa, which made up 6.1% of all the foreign students in the country[7]. Engineering and medicine are mostly popular with students from the Maghreb countries. Medicine and pharmacy appeal to citizens from Arab countries, with 1,378 Moroccans pursuing these degrees in 2012.

It is impossible to promote Russian education into the global market and to prepare foreign specialists unless we teach foreign students how to adapt to the college environment. Under social and cultural adaptation we imply the co-operation between the personality of the foreign student and the new socio-cultural environment. The student has to overcome a number of ethnic, religious, cultural, psychological barriers, getting familiar with the local code of behavior and cultural norms[8].

The adaptation process is a complex and multifaceted one. Arab students have to transform their mindset to adapt to these drastic changes in their lifestyle. It goes hand in hand with stress and psychological pressure, encompassing social and teaching realms. As for the ethno-cultural character of Arab students, they are candid, reasonable, independent, religious, and restless, with high self-esteem but with no skills of working on their own. Also, they are too outgoing, sensitive and moody.

It appears that Arab students from different countries differ in their studying skills. Students from Morocco, Algeria, and Tunisia usually do much better in their studies compared to the students from other Arab countries. The reason behind this is the colonial education system inherited from France. These students know how to read a passage and identify its main idea, are good at note-taking and can work without supervision. It does not

---

[5] Zherlitsina N.A. Perspektivy rossijsko-marokkanskogo sotrudnichestva: potencial i vyzovy [Prospects of Russian-Moroccan cooperation: potential and challenges]. *Vestnik universiteta*, 2015, no. 12, pp. 66-72. P. 67.

[6] Zherlitsina N.A. *Rossijsko-Tunisskie otnoshenija. 1780–1991* [Russian-Tunisian relations. 1780–1991]. Moscow, IAfr RAS, 2014. 216 p. P. 190.

[7] Arefiev A.L., Sheregi F.E. *Inostrannye studenty v rossijskih VUZah* [Foreign students in Russian Universities]. Moscow, TSSI, 2014. 228 p. P. 74.

[8] Chinyaeva T. *Studencheskaja mobil'nost': mirovye tendencii* [Student mobility: global trends]. Visshee obrazovaniye v Rossii, 2002, no. 3, pp. 91-96. P. 94.

take Arab students too long to pick up the Russian language, their listening skills are also impressive. While co-operating with other ethnic groups, Arab students build up self-confidence, becoming more independent and seeking to dominate in inter-personal relations. Ready to speak up their mind, they remain independent in their opinion. Their main objective is to retain their integrity and to protect their national interests. Arab students hate routine and prefer communication. They consider the professor as a communicator who is about to share the information unknown before.

Religion has left its imprint on the education of Arab students. In some Arab countries there are no female teachers, so the students have to get used to female professors. The summer exams or, even worse, the entry exams may fall within Ramadan (a month of exhausting fast where Muslims deprive themselves of food and drink throughout the whole day). This is why it is physically and psychologically demanding for these students to study and pass exams.

Given the socio-cultural and psychological diversity of the student body, it is a pedagogical challenge to help them to adapt. Arab students are rather vulnerable to the problems of social adaptation. Thus, a mere 10% face no problems the first months after coming to Russia. Among the main challenges they mentioned the language barrier, new mode of life, nationalism and racism, blissful ignorance of Russian laws, climate, red-tape in the registration process, security issues. They were also confronted with linguistic and psychological difficulties.

Most of the students are struggling with the language barrier, with 58% complaining that they do not have enough mastery of Russina and only 34.6% considering their command of Russian sufficient to get a degree. The overwhelming majority of 75.3% studied the language at the foundation course in a Russian college whereas a modest 10.9% learnt the Russian language at home[9]. A low command of language has its bearing on the educational process and daily communication alike. It is where students from the same country give a hand to their compatriots, i.e. they help them to learn the language, introduce them to the local friends and just accompany them here and there. Almost a quarter of interviewees mentioned active help from the expatriates communities.

---

[9] Arefiev A.L. *Rossijskie VUZy na mezhdunarodnom rynke obrazovatel'nyh uslug* [Russian universities in the international market of educational services]. Moscow, TSSP, 2007. 487 p. P. 178.

A fully-fledged education requires that a teacher be able to work with a multi-ethnic student body and be aware of the respective ethnic groups, their character and unique features. Most foreign students believe that a cozy atmosphere where they would feel like at home could contribute to the adaptation considerably, with each and every student finding their place. Not least, the composition of groups in foundation courses does matter a lot. A group is usually made of 8–10 people so that a teacher could take care of everybody. It is yet to be agreed whether it is reasonable to follow a one-group nationality approach. I personally believe that a multi-ethnic approach is a better option since, as students put it, this encourages them to learn Russian. Psychologists and sociologists at the foundation course would also benefit in many ways.

Internship is a step on the way to adaptation. Most Arab students struggled to find a job. A mere handful of colleges support their foreign students in job search. In this regard, relevant legal support would be highly appreciated. Students complain about the red-tape, namely "bottleneck with registration", "lame administrative system", "you have to go through numerous offices to get one paper, and never on time" [10].

Their ethnicity "self-drives a wedge between the students and the local population with its local daily routine, which may result in eccentric behavior. A case in point is consumption of their national goods. They decorate their rooms with national flags; opt for national clothes and food products (they refuse to eat pork, keep coffee and spices from their homeland which "are of different quality here"), land listen to national music.

Students have to make a lot of effort to adapt to harsh climate conditions and local food, putting education on the back burner and lagging behind in education. Arab students find it hard to adapt to long and harsh Russian winter with no sun, with late first semester being the hardest. Students get tired, exhausted and depressed, homesick and malnourished due to the lack of fruit and vegetable diversity. It is the point where time comes for a team-building event, a good way to cheer up and relax. The sociological studies show that only one-third of the students get support from the college when it comes to

---

[10] Gribanova V.V., Zherlitsina N.A. *Problemy obuchenija studentov iz afrikanskih stran v VUZah Rossii* [Problems of students from African countries in Russian universities]. *Afrikantsy v Rossiyi: obrazovaniye, brak, semya*. Moscow, IAfr RAS, 2009, pp.48 -55. P. 52.

leisure activities[11], with most support coming from Moscow colleges. Among the widely-spread leisure activities are dating nights, discos, concerts, intellectual competitions, comedy clubs and sports competitions. It goes without saying that national and religious parties also serve an educational purpose. Foreign students get familiar with Russian modes of behaviour, customs, way of life, perceptions of history and religion. Museums, exhibitions, concerts, theatres, international parties – all of these contribute to mutual understanding.

The main challenge confronting Arab students is the attitude of the local people. The process of cultural co-operation may still be found difficult, as a result of the former iron curtain and a lack of experience in communicating with foreigners. The shortage of information and cultural clashes contribute to the spooky image of the "stranger". The more negative the connotation that is attributed to the image, the wider the gap created by mutual mistrust, tensions and fear. With Russians being inert and foreign students unprepared to adapt, conflict situations may occur and further impede the educational process.

A positive trend is that over the last decades the process of adaptation has become a great deal easier: with telecommunications enabling students to keep in touch with the family, better service sector and transport facilitating climate adaptation, mushrooming Oriental shops, cafes and restaurants. Thus, students have opportunity to watch national and international satellite TV-channels installed on campus, and to listen to national the radio station on a regular basis.

Ignorant of Russian conditions and lacking in information, Arab students experience much fewer difficulties when supported by administrative staff in charge for foreign students. Russia is yet to design a universal guide for foreign students, translated into different world languages and accessible for anyone who is considering a Russian education. World leaders in the higher education market issue a range of such guides and circulate them across the globe.

In conclusion, the Russian education of foreign students dates back to over 100 years ago and rests on a well-developed and internationally recognised higher education. In the education market, however, Russian higher education is facing new challenges which require modern approaches and innovative decisions.

---

[11] Noskova S.V. *Obucheniye inostrannikh studentov v rossiyskikh vuzakh: spetsifika i prognozi* [Training of foreign students in Russian universities: the specificity and forecasts]. *Obrazovaniye dliya vsekh: puti integratsii.* Saratov, SGTU, 2003. P. 43.

Vladimir Pavlov

BRICS: CHINA'S NEW MODELS FOR STIMULATING ECONOMIC DEVELOPMENT AND MODERNIZATION IN THE LEAST DEVELOPED COUNTRIES OF AFRICA[1]

China's active participation in BRICS equips it with a number of significant advantages and opportunities, notably:
– carrying out large-scale transnational initiatives that can raise China's profile in the development and implementation of global reforms of international economic relations and international finance;
– further strengthening of China's position as the most important global player of the world economy;
– increasing the role of the country's rapidly developing economy in the context of growing South-South cooperation; there is a significant expansion of military-technical cooperation with South Africa and Brazil. Military-technical cooperation within BRICS is based primarily on bilateral agreements;
– progressively reforming the national system of economic governance and foreign economic relations;
– boosting trade and investment cooperation with the BRICS members and other developing countries;
– directly participating in the development of global reforms in the field of international development, international economic exchange, and international finance;
– constructing and implementing qualitatively new models of economic development in developing countries, including the least developed ones.

China has proclaimed its desire to intensify South-South cooperation and expand North-South dialogue within the framework of achieving the Millennium Development Goals in order to strengthen the positions of developing countries in the world economy and system of global economic governance, and to increase their potential in combating all forms of protectionism in international economic relations.

BRICS provides China with additional opportunities to withstand the growing US hegemony in the world economy without confronting the current

---

[1] First published in the collection *BRICS in the Year of the 7th Summit: Focus on Africa*. Moscow, Institute for African Studies, RAS, 2015, pp. 99-111.

US administration directly[2]. In 2013–2015, China's top priority within the framework of BRICS was to deepen direct ties with emerging and rapidly developing markets, as well as with so-called "frontier markets" (markets that are close in their basic characteristics and parameters to rapidly emerging markets). This objective largely reflects the global nature of China's economic interests. In our view, the desire to strengthen regulatory relations and foreign economic exchange with this group of developing countries explains many of China's purposeful actions in the international arena in 2010–2015, including:

– strengthening the position of South Africa as a full member of BRICS;

– intensifying investment expansion in Africa;

– facilitating the transformation of the countries of Southern Africa into a catalyst of the sustainable development of the rest of the continent;

– taking measures to reduce the impact of the IBSA Dialogue Forum (India, Brazil, South Africa) on the development of the African continent since this economic grouping, based on the common economic and, to a considerable extent, political identity of these three countries, all of which are at a certain level of development of democratic society and have rapidly growing large and lucrative domestic markets, has deliberately excluded the possibility of membership or any other involvement of China;

– vigorously proposing the creation of a permanent BRICS secretariat since 2013;

– appointing a group of highly qualified Chinese banking professionals, who had previously contributed decisively to the development and diversification of China's domestic lending market, to the BRICS New Development Bank. A representative of China is expected to become the permanent chair of the Bank's Board of Directors;

– increasing the role of the state in supporting the foreign expansion of Chinese capital and internationalisation of Chinese companies – primarily of state-owned enterprises (SOEs), and in facilitating international trade growth and China's foreign direct investment;

– strengthening direct bilateral relations with specific developing countries – exporters of mineral resources, timber, and energy resources (in the context of the policy of ensuring the security of China's energy sector on the

---

[2] Abdenur A.E. China and the BRICS Development Bank: Legitimacy and Multilateralism in South-South Cooperation. *Institute of Development Studies*, 2014, vol. 45, no. 4, pp. 85-102.

basis of the diversification of energy suppliers and intensification of South–South economic and political cooperation).

In 2014–2015, without any preconditions, demands, and obligations China strove to introduce (primarily in Africa) new principles and models of long-term development in the framework of its basic concept of intensifying the horizontal economic integration of national economies of developing countries and the formation of transboundary development corridors.

The 2013 White Paper of the State Council of China, "China–Africa Trade and Economic Cooperation", testifies that these "models for the formation of a higher-performing economy" and facilitation of the emergence of rapidly developing markets in the region are based on the eight main principles proclaimed by the then Premier of the State Council of the People's Republic of China Zhou Enlai in the 1960s. From a political perspective, this concept, which was designed to counter the perception of China in the modern world as a leader that threatened other world powers and to improve its foreign policy image, is understood as the idea of a "peaceful rise". It has also been referred to as "peaceful development". This idea is inextricably linked with China's current strategy of employing "soft power" in diplomatic relations, educational programmes, and cultural ties with African countries. In financial terms, this strategy is effectively combined with strategic grants, soft preferential loans (at subsidised interest rates), official development assistance (ODA) and the influx of Chinese public and private investment capitals into African countries.

In line with the implementation of this strategy, the state also facilitates the establishment of closer direct ties between China's civil society organisations and partners and counterparts from African countries. In the long term, until 2020, the Chinese government will apparently continue to pursue the policy of expanding direct financial assistance, including ODA, mutual trade, and the flow of direct Chinese industrial and private investment in African countries. China will also continue to expand the availability of various types of loans at market interest rates, intensify preferential lending at subsidised below-market interest rates, provide targeted grants to African states, and restructure, write off, or fully cancel their external public debt.

Chinese models of accelerating the development and modernisation of African economies, in our estimation, also take into account both positive and negative experience of internal economic reforms and social transformations in China during the rule of Deng Xiaoping, and their factual results.

The essence of these models (with unconditional consideration of the economic and political peculiarities of specific African countries – recipients of long-term Chinese investment capital) is reduced to the mandatory inclusion of basic standardised provisions, requirements, and schemes for regulating national economies and domestic financial markets – especially the institutional banking sector – in the state economic programmes and development plans of the recipient African countries. The most important of these provisions are:

– persistent strengthening of the role of the state in the national economy at the initial stage, including by stimulating the development of the public sector and increasing the capital of SOEs (in the energy, mining, manufacturing, and financial sectors, especially in the national banking sector, etc.);

– improving public administration systems and transiting to the project-oriented method of economic governance and building modern institutions in the course of modernisation in African countries;

– implementing comprehensive step-by-step economic liberalisation in agrarian and rural areas, as well as in local small-scale industrial (artisanal) production;

– creating special (free, export, open, etc.) economic zones (SEZs) in order to stimulate a steady inflow of foreign investment and transfer of more modern technologies to African countries;

– establishing transboundary investment corridors and areas of intensive development with a view to increasing the inflow of foreign direct investment and significantly enhancing the horizontal integration of bordering and neighbouring African countries, including with a view to deepening their industrial, trade, and marketing cooperation and increasing their aggregate export potential (on the basis of synergies of their multilateral horizontal cooperation and integration);

– providing state support and incentives for industrial investment (including through raising finance from external sources) in large-scale projects in the sector of hard infrastructure: construction of dams, irrigation systems, paved roads, highways (including international), railways, ports, industrial complexes, urban facilities, etc. in the context of stimulating a steady increase in the capitalisation of SOEs and increasing their production capacity;

– gradually expanding the private sector of the economy, especially its national African segment, also in order to reduce poverty and misery, through fiscal and lending incentives for local small and medium-sized private entrepreneurship (in the segments of trade, services, local small industrial and cooperative production)[3];

– carrying out "cautious", balanced, and rational political liberalisation that would take into account the dramatically increasing migration of population between rural areas and developing urban areas and agglomerations and further increases in the total number of "permanently floating" migrants (citizens of working age regularly moving from rural settlements to cities and back), which lead to a steady increase in the scale of interregional migration in many African countries.

The identification of the most important sources and optimal methods of financing development, including the search for new resources to attract additional investment capital and finance deficits, has come to occupy the most important place in modern diversified Chinese models of transition to higher-performing national economies in African countries. The methods, which supposedly have been effectively adapted to contemporary African realities, include the following:

– drawing on the experience of China, which has achieved the dynamic development of the national economy, it is proposed to begin financing development with the establishment and increasing the capitalisation of state-owned banking institutions or state-controlled development banks specially created for day-to-day support and sustainable financing of long-term domestic investments in the country, including the involvement of national systemically important banks (political banks) in the investment process. In China, these banks are, first of all, the China Development Bank (CDB) and the Export–Import Bank of China (China Exim Bank – CEB). Established in 1994, CDB provides long-term loans for financing large hard infrastructure projects. CDB describes itself as "an engine that provides electricity to the national policy of economic development". The bank has established and maintains regular contact with relevant government agencies. The current chief executive officer of CDB is a member of the Council of Ministers of China. CDB operates under the direct jurisdiction of the State Council of China. Large hard infrastructure projects that CDB financed have led to significant positive changes in the country's economic and social development. Many large-scale Chinese projects abroad generate higher sustainable profits for SOEs and private companies than their domestic incomes. As a result, deve-

---

[3] Greenhill R., Prizzon F., Rogerson F. *The Age of Choice: Developing Countries in the New Aid Landscape.* L., 2013, pp. 121-128.

lopment banks increasingly mediate and finance Chinese investments abroad, primarily private ones.

According to Chinese experts, the emphasis on state-owned development banks (both specialised and universal multisectoral ones) in financing economic development does not discard the greater engagement of sub-regional development banks in Africa, mostly by increasing their liquidity and capitalisation. These include: the West African Development Bank, the Development Bank of the Central African States, the East African Development Bank, and the Development Bank of the States of Great Lakes. However, according to our assessment, the current financial situation of these banks is unsustainable; national budget deficits in the participating countries do not allow them to replenish the subscribed share capital of these banks, so the latter face an increase in overdue unpaid receivables. For these reasons, a noticeable growth of their regular lending operations is unlikely in the short term. Under present conditions, only an influx of foreign capital (both public and private), including from China and other BRICS countries (India, Brazil) will be able to ensure an increase in the volume of their lending operations and investment project financing;

– using foreign aid, expanding non-traditional export trade, providing the most favourable conditions for the inflow of foreign entrepreneurial capital, including private one, obtaining and using loans (both at market and subsidised interest rates), increasing the influx of external grants, seeking to cancel external debt partly or in full, countries of the region should pursue efforts to establish designated (special) economic zones, including transboundary ones, within the multi-country zones and investment corridors of more intense development that are emerging in Africa. These zones include: special export zones, special industrial and technological zones, technological zones, venture investment capital zones, tourist zones, industrial production zones, etc. In their recommendations, Chinese experts usually stress the need to prioritise the establishment of new free economic zones, free export zones, and, less often, free industrial zones in order to raise economic productivity and introduce project-oriented management in countries of the continent.

It is also recommended that African countries adapt the basic elements of China's experience in the creation of designated and special economic zones to the present African realities and more intensively introduce the "results of Chinese research in this field" into their economic fabric[4]. At the same time,

---

[4] Mawdsley E. *From Recipients to Donors: Emerging Powers and the Changing Development Landscape.* L., 2012, pp. 40-42.

however, countries of Africa are warned against attempting to implement fundamental trade reforms based on the Chinese model, in particular against transferring models of reorganisation of domestic wholesale trade and other trade reforms developed in China to the African soil;

– growth of capital and diversification of local commercial banks in Africa, drawing on the experience gained by China's state-owned and private commercial banks in 2010–2015 (diversified credit lines, the use of grants, new models for securing interbank credit swaps, repaying loans under previously opened lines of credit, the ability to repay bank loans with local products and primary commodities).

What is the key, however, is that the countries of the region are strongly encouraged to support local commercial banks, including private and collective ones (in particular, by granting them tax incentives and preferences and implementing other fiscal measures), so that these banks purposefully expand market lending (at market interest rates) and project financing in the sector of hard (essential) infrastructure and within the framework of national industrial policies. Projects with the participation of foreign investors, shareholders, and donors should also be included. In addition, local African commercial banks should expand the practice of co-financing such projects in cooperation with foreign investors, banks, and funds. In the latter case, African banks (as well as local African companies) should identify areas of the national economy that have potential for sustainable growth. Moreover, they should directly assume higher risks than foreign banks and private non-resident investors[5]:

– each African country should establish a single authorised coordinating body for attracting financial and technical assistance (including ODA), as well as other sources of external investment financing (including interbank lending), foreign grants, interest-free concessional and non-concessional loans, export loans, loans from multilateral international lending institutions and funds; this body should also be empowered to revoke and cancel projects of foreign investors and shareholders planned for implementation in Africa;

– African countries should establish new, and facilitate operations of previously established, state-owned agricultural development banks, including by stimulating the inflow of foreign public and private capital, with the possibility of their gradual transformation into commercial (private) structures;

– a closer link should be maintained between the nation state and the domestic commodity market in order to embed the state into "economic fabric"

---

[5] Moyo D. *Dead Aid: Why Aid is Not Working and How There is a Better Way for Africa.* Vancouver, 2009, pp. 171-176.

with a view to gradually forming regular trade and domestic financial markets (which primarily integrate domestic lending markets, securities markets, and foreign exchange markets) in the countries of the region;

– a special focus should be made on more intensive attraction of Chinese investment to the region, as well as investment from other BRICS countries. Meanwhile, this particular investment model has now acquired some objective basic parameters and key characteristics reminiscent of the French and British expansion in Africa in the colonial era. However, the dynamics of China's investment strategy in Africa (and in developing countries in general) in 2013–2015 can be characterised by growing flexibility, versatility, comprehensive analysis of socio-political conditions in specific recipient countries, and subsequent revision of the strategy (including the training of skilled technicians and workers, provision of social benefits, bonuses, and subsidies to employees of industrial facilities in sectors of the economy with the participation of Chinese capital, etc.);

– in view of China's desire to expand its equity participation in international financial development organisations, the long-term goal is revitalising the African Development Bank (AfDB) and transforming it into an essential element of Africa's aggregate lending market in the context of diversifying sources of financing African countries' development and increasing AfDB's own capitalisation. This approach reflects a balanced and prudent strategy of acting in accordance with the Chinese proverb "crossing the river by feeling for stones". Moreover, proceeding from the officially announced national priority task of "helping developing countries and reducing poverty in the modern world", China is now expanding its equity participation in AfDB, as shown in Table 1.

Table 1

Subscriptions by the BRICS member countries and their voting power on 31 December 2012 (amounts in millions of AfDB's units of account)[6]

Member States	Total Shares	% of Total Shares	Number of Votes	% of Total Voting Power
Brazil	28,084	0.445	28,710	0.452
India	14,183	0.225	14,808	0.233
China	70,920	1.124	71,545	1.126
South Africa	305,208	4.838	305,833	4.811

* Russia is not a member state of AfDB or other institutions of its Group (2017).

---

[6]*African Development Bank Annual Report 2012.* Tunis, 2012, pp. 127-130.

Since the mid-1980s, China has been an active participant of the African Development Bank and the African Development Fund (ADF). It has signed special target agreements with AfDB on financing environmental protection programmes, agricultural development, water supply, and public health in African countries. The China Development Bank and the Export–Import Bank of China (China Exim Bank) have signed Memoranda of Understanding with AfDB. China's total contribution to AfDB capital went from the initial $14.59 million to $486 million. In 2013–2014, China started to put into practice a new mechanism of co-financing with AfDB to ensure long-term financing of hard infrastructure projects and to support initiatives and targeted programmes for the acceleration of private sector growth in African countries.

In the coming years (until 2020), the New Development Bank will prioritise its lending operations not only in the BRICS countries, but also in Africa. The experience that leading Chinese banks have accumulated in the region will enable the bank to strengthen its cooperation with African regional banks and development funds.

In practice, the new mechanism for co-financing large-scale investment projects and poverty eradication programmes by Chinese banks, AfDB, and ADF will assist Chinese private capital to invest in prioritised sectors of the economies of recipient African countries[7].

In general, the formation of a new model of development of African countries, which provides for the growing influence of Chinese capital on the economies of the recipient countries of the region, and China's support for AfDB and the co-financing mechanism give impetus to the gradual transition of the countries of the region to a more productive economy. AfDB has become the key element of Africa's emerging lending market. Due to the growing weakness of African credit and banking structures, the impact of AfDB on the development of the real sector of Africa's transition economies and the processes of sectoral diversification has increased. Through the attraction of additional external financing and the proliferation of the mechanism of co-financing with leading international credit organisations and funds, in particular with leading Chinese development banks, AfDB gains additional resources for the modernisation of the economies of the continent and occasionally strengthens their positions in world com-

---

[7] Mwase N., Yang Y. *BRICs' Philosophies for Development Financing and Their Implications for LICs.* IMF. Wash., DC, 2012, pp. 5-8.

modity markets. As for the recommendations for improving national monetary policies of African countries, China highlights the need to introduce the basic principles of a long-term economic strategy, more specifically, the policy mix, which aims to combine the most effective methods and instruments of a country's monetary and fiscal policies on the basis of strengthening cooperation and coordination between a country's Central Bank and its Ministry of Finance. It is often admitted, however, that such a mechanism can now be successfully implemented only in relatively few African countries, mostly in West Africa. In this connection, the experience of Nigeria in implementing the policy mix in 2010–2015 is generally recognised as sufficiently effective and can be repeated in many countries of Africa. This view is held by the U.S. administration, in particular the U.S. Department of State.

As for the practical application of methods and instruments of liberal monetary policy in African countries, it is primarily a matter of refraining from the economically unjustifiable containment of monetary expansion (M0, M1, and M2 types of money supply), decreasing commercial interest rates and the refinancing rate of the Central Bank, and reducing the minimum amount of reserves (reserve requirement) that must be held by a commercial bank in the Central Bank.

In the framework of the new model of economic development of Africa, most countries of the region, including South Africa, are strongly encouraged to intensify:

– import of goods and services;

– contractor and subcontractor construction and development activities;

– teaching, training, and retraining of skilled workers and technicians (technical personnel);

– the inflow of Chinese direct industrial investment;

– transfer of technologies and sharing of scientific and technological knowledge;

– other forms of cooperation.

From the economic (financial) point of view, China does not seek to further increase its investment in Africa, in particular, because recipient countries offer no real opportunities for sustainable high returns on investment (net profits). However, its African initiatives are likely to expand with a view to gain additional benefits and advantages. At the same time, most of these benefits are more political than economic. China's effort to strengthen its role in the South-South multilateral system of cooperation will continue. China's Africa policy, as well as its activities in the framework of the New Development Bank, will continue to be subordinated to the goal of increasing China's political weight as a key global player.

The total volume of China's cooperation with all developing countries now by far exceeds the corresponding figures of most leading powers in the world, including other BRICS countries. Direct economic benefits from the intensive financing of hard infrastructure industries (often with an emphasis on facilitating intensive growth of hard infrastructure in a mixed transition economy) are not as obvious as previously thought[8]. In a weak economy which may be experiencing declining economic growth rates, the development of hard infrastructure through medium and large investment projects often does not produce the desired results and is unreasonably expensive. In principle, the key idea that the priority construction of paved roads, dams, bridges, seaports, etc. will increase labour productivity in a country is true, but it often does not lead to the desired outcome.

China is now striving to develop and implement innovative ways and mechanisms that will link the development of hard infrastructure, the processes of industrialisation, and the modernisation of mixed transition economies directly to the fight against poverty, hunger, and misery in developing countries.

As part of China's long-term investment strategy in developing countries, new fundamental issues, which previously were not considered relevant or of significant importance, have been included in the agenda, such as: human rights, the right to work, working conditions, environmental protection, and other aspects of social well-being of the population in developing countries. Another new important aspect of this strategy is the development of civil society. It this connection, China facilitates the development of networks of non-governmental organisations, professional associations, non-profit organisations, national communities organisations, diaspora associations, etc. in recipient countries.

China seeks to significantly expand the range of forms and methods of project financing which are adapted to the realities of Asian and African countries and which international banks and development funds with equity participation of BRICS countries could make accessible to the least developed countries with the lowest per capita income, thus counterbalancing the present lending practices of banking institutions controlled by industrialised countries and the IMF.

---

[8]Pavlov V.V., Klishin V.V. *The African Development Bank: Financial Strategies for Modernising Economies of African Countries.* Moscow, 2015, pp. 52-57.

Anatoly Savateev

PROPHETS OF ISLAM IN TROPICAL AFRICA – THE FATHERS OF CIVILIZATIONAL IDENTITY[1]

Civilizational identity stands for the highest and the most general level of human consciousness, which blends together basic perception of life purpose, deep connection with Divine and ways of communicating with others, moral code of behaviour, political system, notions of beauty and ugliness through the lens of eternal truth. The core element of a civilizational identity is cultural consciousness, which is inextricably bound up with the social base and usually manifests itself as religious commitment. Therefore a civilizational consciousness is influenced by religion in the first place. A graphic example here is self-consciousness and behaviour within the Muslim community in contemporary Sub-Saharan Africa.

When and how did the Islamic civilizational consciousness come to exist on the African continent? What are the origins of Sub-Saharan religious and civilizational identity? Is it not an exaggeration to assume that Islamic civilization emerged in this part of Africa? After all, the sub-region is seemingly dominated by African traditional culture and beliefs. Is it possible to forecast a scenario for further establishment of Afro-Islamic or Islamic-African civilization?

A decisive factor here, which made the Islamic civilization and Islamic identity possible, is a plethora of prominent personalities, i.e. self-proclaimed prophets of jihad in the 19th–early 20th centuries.

Back in those days, Sub-Saharan Africa witnessed an Islamic prophesy "explosion" unknown to this part of the world ever before. The development of the African branch of Islamic civilization (8th–18th centuries) underlay the phenomenon of prophesy gathering pace in the region. It emerged, firstly, as a response to the growth of Muslim spiritual schools' (such as *Tariqas*, brotherhoods); secondly, as a revolt against "faithless authorities" that brought injustice, economic exploitation, infringements of freedom and insulting dignity through humiliation. This protest took the form of *jihad* ("sacred war") aimed at overthrowing "non-Islamic rulers" and converting all the peoples on

---

[1] First published in the collection *Searches of Identity in World History and Culture*. Yaroslavl, Demidov Yaroslavl State University, 2014, pp. 27-34.

the continent to the religion of the Prophet Muhammad, establishing a community of fellow believers to live in line with Islam.

These ideas were brought to the table by spiritual leaders who managed to transcend the borders of reality and who believed that they were the messengers of Muhammad and that their mission was to profess to Africans. They turned their focus towards proclaiming Sharia law, i.e. a setting of religious, legal, moral, cultural, political rules. Among those charismatic leaders are the Fulani religious revolutionary Usman dan Fodiyo[2, 3], the Toucouleur preacher and warrior El-Hadj Omar , the Sudanese *Mahdi* (messenger of Allah) Muhamad Ahmad, a staunch leader of the revolt against non-Muslims in Somalia Muhammad Abdille Hassan, a Senegalese silent resistance leader Amadu Bamba and anti-western leader in Nigeria Muhammad Marva (Maitatsine). They all stood out for their devout religiosity and knowledge of Islamic science and social philosophy. Being gifted in literature and eloquent public speakers, these leaders deeply believed they were chosen by God. Deep social penetration of passionate preaching and an insight into hopes and aspirations of new converts helped them to enlist numerous followers. This is how new spiritual religious communities appeared (*jamaat*), with a prophet's pivotal figure as a spiritual and military leader, "Father of the Faithful".

Being mostly warriors, these prophets conducted "*jihad of the sword*" (i.e military struggle), with the exception of the preacher Amadou Bamba[4], whose peaceful *jihad of the heart*" (struggle with personal sins) left its trace in the history national consciousness and souls of not only of Senegal but of a large part of West Africa.

What was the mission of Islamic prophets? Firstly, appearing when society and government were on the brink of a crisis, they responded to a public desire for a saviour, a charismatic leader capable of leading to a break in the deadlock. Secondly, they could unite African Muslims together with common

---

[2] Savateev A.D. A treatise by Osman dan Fodio as a historical and cultural phenomenon of Islamic civilization. *D.A. Olderogge and contemporary African studies in Russia. The conference after D.A. Olderogge "Africa: societies, cultures, languages' (7-9 October 2003, Saint-Petersburg).* Moscow, 2005.

[3] Savateev A.D. Religiozno-politicheskie sochinenija Osmana dan Fodio – istochnik dlja ponimanija istorii Zapadnoj Afriki [Religious and Political Works of Usman dan Fodio as a Source for West African History Comprehension. *Vostok (Oriens),* 2006, no. 1, pp. 53-64.

[4] Coulon Ch. *Prophets of God or of History? Muslim Messianic Movements and Anti-colonialism in Senegal.* Theoretic Explorations in African Religion. London, KPI, 1985, pp. 346-351.

cultural, moral, religious, political ideas to shape an Islamic African civilization that shares the same social and cultural values. It was Islam that fuelled revolutionary sentiment, which set the boundaries of social and cultural space. Thirdly, these "small prophets" became visionaries who ran massive resistance against the European colonizers at the very outset of the Western colonisation in Tropical Africa. The struggle became a continuation of the prophetic movement – although Osman dan Fodio's jihad occurred when future colonial states were only considering the conquest of the Black Continent. Lastly, the most important mission of the prophets was not just to establish a state but to lay the civilizational basis for a set of spiritual and cultural principles, ideas and concepts.

As Muslims see it, the prophets have five features in common: they are (1) truthful; (2) committed, since they are people of honour; (3) capable of understanding and spreading the law of God; (4) high-brow intellectuals; (5) impeccably pure in thought and free of sinful behaviour.

The Prophet Muhammad is considered to be a role model[5]. His consistent resistance, unexpected retirement and further comeback set a par for "small" prophets in Tropical Africa who bid defiance to the current order and pursued a new one. The life of Muhammad was the yardstick for Osman dan Fodio, the leader of the Fulani revolt, Muhammad Ahmed the leader of the Sudanese *Mahdi* expansion movement and Al-Hajj Omar.

Originally, the teaching of Muhammad was supposed to put aside one of the main existential controversies – the one between the personal individuality closely-knit with the mother-nature, limited in time and in space and a human being as a Divine creature, inherent part of the eternal and unlimited universe. The instructions of the Prophet appealed to the individual rather than to society, demanding believers to make a personal, intellectual, and moral effort, as well as a certain mindset and political choice[6].

To enter the Muslim establishment one must be a well-educated person with a keen understanding of the Scripture who ideally is able to create original sacred texts as well. This is why these people are also known as "*scribes*". The mechanism of shaping the spiritual leaders perpetuated itself. In terms of culture and society, Muslim prophets were relatively independent from and even superior to political, military and economic leaders. In fact,

---

[5] Lewis B. *Islam and the West*. Moscow, the Institute of Scripture and Theology, 2003.

[6] Savateev A.D. *Islamskaja civilizacija v Tropicheskoj Afrike* [Islamic civilization in sub-Saharan Africa]. Moscow, Institute for African Studies RAS, 2006, pp. 50-51.

they were expected to become ad hoc political and military leaders. Usually the role of the military jihad leader, i.e. military leaders, was taken by spiritual and religious leaders – prophetic personalities in Islam. Amadou Bamba, the founder of the Muslim order called Muridiya (the Mourid Brotherhood), a school which gained popularity in Senegal and abroad afterwards – was something else entirely.

Since the 18th century Islamic civilization has been shaping people's spirituality in Sub-Saharan Africa. The Muslim traditional establishment under the guidance of a charismatic prophet maintained spiritual standards throughout a large new-found territory, inhabited by various peoples which often belong to several states. These prophets made it possible to reach a high spiritual and cultural level, as well as to incorporate common religious and secular (in their essence) norms into society.

Proliferating across Sub-Saharan Africa, Wahabbi ideas contributed to the religious and political implosion in the Muslim society and to the development of jihad movements. In the opinion of many Western authors, the Wahabbi movement left an imprint on a range of jihad leaders in West Africa. For example Sheik al-Hadj Omar and Seku Ahmadu Lobbo were reluctant to adopt Wahabbi principles since they contradicted Suffi ones; these leaders, however, managed to "find in Wahabbism a belief that *jihad* is a way of religious renaissance"[7]. This evidence testifies to the fact that religion and spirituality brought together an array of Muslims in tropical Africa into a community (the *Umma*). At meetings of the *umma* they caught up with the world news such as the Crimean War and the assassination of the general Gordon by the warriors of Mahdi[8].

The activity of Islamic prophets in Sub-Saharan Africa yielded tangible results, nurturing a sense of belonging to Islamic civilization. D.R. Willis, an American expert on African Islam, illustrated this change with the example of the movement of El-Hadj Omar as follows: "*Jinamaat* (community) Omara offered Islam as a source of new cultural identity to all people at a loss, irrespective of their origin. Islam and new Islamic community came to replace previous networks as this new faith seemed superior to traditional be-

---

[7] Willis J.R. *Introduction: Reflections on the Diffusion of Islam in West Africa.* Studies in West African Islamic History, vol. 1 (The Cultivators of Islam). L., Frank Cass, 1979. P. 31,

[8] Hiskett M. *The Development of Islam in West Africa.* L.–N.Y., Longman, 1984. P. 224.

liefs and strict compliance with the Islamic law ensured higher social status"[9].

The popularity of a prophetic movement– whether it is *jihad* of the sword or *jihad* of the heart – correlated with the commitment and abilities of a prophetic movement leader. For instance, it took Sudanese *Mahdi* Muhammad Ahmed a mere 4 years to drive the Egyptians and the British across the border. He later meticulously designed the principles of an Islamic theocratic state, guidelines for relations between the state and believers, for their respective freedoms and responsibilities.

Likewise, peaceful *jihad* led by Amadou Bamba yielded impressive results. With no military conquest, he managed to establish Tariqa Muridiya, the only Tariqa that took the form of a sub-civilizational project and is still up and running. Owing to the principles laid over 100 years ago, it still exists and successfully adapts to changing social and political conditions, regulations of international and domestic order. Sheik Amadou Bamba, who was declared a saint even before his death, designed his own system of labour division, education, and solidarity. All in all, Tariqas of the19th–20th centuries triggered religious revolution that is still a source of civilizational identity for African Muslims.

The questions on the personality of self-proclaimed prophets who gathered tens of thousands of followers suggest defining whose will did these prophets follow. From the religious perspective, the answer is that they executed the will of God, an answer most Muslims could unanimously agree with. However, from the civilizational perspective, prophets are shapers of destinies, who create the great dome of Islamic civilization in Sub-Saharan Africa.

---

[9] Willis J.R. Jihad fi Sabil Allah – Its Doctrinal Basis in Islam and Some Aspects of its Evolution in Nineteenth Century West Africa. *Journal of African History*, 1967, vol. VIII, no. 3. P. 400.

Alexey Vasiliev

ARAB REVOLUTIONS AND THE PROTEST MOVEMENT: CAUSES, DRIVING FORCES, AND RESULTS[1]

What caused the Arab revolutions and protest movements? The answer is seemingly obvious: these were revolts against repressive regimes, autocracy, and corruption; their cause is rooted in the absence of freedoms, in the poverty of populations, and in the colossal gap between rich and poor. However, the situation in the Arab states was far from being the worst; at the beginning of this century, their economies developed at a faster pace than the world's average. GDP growth in Egypt was 5–7%, a figure testifying to advance. Tunisia was the most prosperous country on the African continent. Libya literally rolled in oil money and was famous for its free education and healthcare, practically free accommodation, and excellent roads. As for repressions and corruption, the situation in many non-Arab countries was much more difficult.

What led to the explosion? The point is that, at one moment or another, a critical mass of people's wrath accumulated, and a psychological atmosphere of antagonism to authoritarian regimes was formed, especially with regard to those headed by aged leaders and fuddy-duddy elites. In the majority of the continent's countries, people began to ask themselves: why do non-Europeans – the Japanese, then the Koreans, and now the Chinese – live increasingly better and become increasingly more powerful, while we remain in this deplorable state? The answer was as follows: the rulers and the existing system are to blame. The dissatisfaction of the masses manifested itself in the slogan "Enough!" By the way, one of the small protest parties used this word as its self-designation (*Kefaya!*).

However, there appeared still another circumstance, or, to be more precise, a special demographic situation developed in which the young constituted the larger part of the population. To designate such situations, sociology uses the term *youth bulge*. The demographic misbalance in the Arab countries resulted from the fact that, 20–30 years earlier, owing to achievements in medicine, child mortality had decreased, while female fertility (the number of births per woman) remained the same. In the majority of the Arab countries,

---

[1]First published in *Herald of the Russian Academy of Sciences*. Vol. 84, Issue 3, 2014.

many sufficiently educated young people have grown up, who use computers, mobile telephones, and other instruments of state-of-the-art information technologies. However, they have no future, no "social lift," as the phrase goes. They are passionate and ready to take to the streets, to protest, and to seek a better life. These young people had no recognized leaders; however, using new information technologies and, sometimes, owing to personal heroism, they managed to stir the masses against the existing regimes.

Yet the countries of the Arab world are different in many respects. Among them are both the poorest states on our planet, such as Yemen and Mauritania, and the richest countries where the GDP per capita is two-to-three times higher than in the United States (Qatar and the United Arab Emirates). Among them are monarchies and republics; countries with strong tribal traditions and countries where these traditions have been forgotten. There are the Sunni and the Shia. For these reasons protest movements and revolutions in these countries developed differently.

Some people have tried to find external influences in the current events and lean toward conspiracy theories, according to which behind-the-scenes forces in the United States and Western Europe worked everything out in advance and have been preparing Islamists to replace the liberal youth. I am an adversary of conspiracy theory because I am sure that there are neither groups nor individuals who could work out all the consequences in advance for the coming years and decades and control the process. Moreover, if we speak about the position of the United States and its role in the region in question, we should take into consideration that it wanted reforms rather than revolutions. Washington understood that social disasters and rebellions were possible there and tried to inculcate in the ruling elites the necessity to change the situation and to implement reforms. There even appeared the US Greater Middle East Program. The American message to the local ruling elites meant that it was necessary for them to introduce changes and reforms from the top down. However, these attempts failed, and protest movements continued to grow.

Everything began in Tunisia, a relatively well-to-do country. Note, however, that the local youth had no future either. A policewoman insulted a well-educated young man, who had unwillingly become a peddler, and he set himself on fire using a flammable mixture and died in terrible agony. This living torch, one can say, lit the fire of revolution. Tunisia and Egypt are direct allies of the United States, and Washington hoped at first that it would be possible to save H. Mubarak; Israel was interested in securing his regime because this meant that the peace treaty would remain effective.

However, the protests were so strong that Washington changed its policy and actually sacrificed Mubarak. The military seized power. What could follow, however? Democracy? Freedom? Human rights? New power? When some of the Western principles came in use, it became clear that they fell on an unfit civilizational soil, where Western ideas were alien to the majority of the population.

Over the last 200 years, a dualism of civilizations has been developing in the Arab countries. On the one hand, market (let us call them capitalist, pro-Western) structures and forms of activity have been evolving; on the other, traditional communities, tribes, religious communities, and sects have survived, as well as a typical Arab mentality. The new live at the expense of the old.

In these circumstances, many people seek protection by hiding themselves behind the shell of religious customs, beliefs, and connections. They believe that the Golden Age of Islam existed at some point, and the present difficulties of the Arab peoples are not because they have not modernized themselves but rather because they have rejected their native values. The Muslim Brotherhood movement has appeared, embracing now about 80 Muslim countries. Its slogans are "The Quran Is Our Constitution", "Islam Is the Solution", etc. The "Brothers" promised radical changes, yet without outlining how to solve the problems. People believed them.

Recently, Egypt has four times carried out elections and referenda, invariably won by the Muslim Brothers: in voting on the constitution, in parliament elections, and in presidential elections. As a result, an Islamic president came to power, although by a slender margin. Islamists came to power in Tunisia as well. What could the Americans, who had allegedly planned everything in advance, do in these circumstances? They decided to negotiate with the Islamists so as to protect the treaty with Israel and to preserve the West's economic positions in the region. The traditions of such cooperation were established in the 1950s–1970s on the basis of anti-Soviet and anticommunist activity aimed against secular anti-Western regimes.

Washington began cooperating with the Islamist president of Egypt. The United States helped him to normalize somehow Egypt's relations with Israel and to prevent a military operation in Gaza. Remember that power in Gaza belongs to Hamas, which is practically the Muslim Brotherhood's affiliate. In general, Palestine–Israeli relations are a colossal topic, deserving a separate discussion.

What next? All revolutions in history have always led to economic decline. Then the way is cleaned, and the economy revives. However, the masses expect that a revolution will immediately bring prosperity, but this does not happen. The economic situation worsens everywhere, investment ceases to come, capital flees, and the number of tourists becomes smaller and smaller. Revolutionaries, of course, promise much and believe that, for example, they will be able to return all the money taken out by corrupt officials to the West. No, stolen money does not come back, and the life of the masses becomes even worse.

The Islamists who had come to power had no political experience and failed to find compromises. In a determined manner they promoted their people to senior positions in ministries, universities, and mass media. *Brothers* are *al-ikhwån* in Arabic. Mass *ikhwanization* of the state apparatus and mass media started. Intolerable errors were made. For example, a representative of the extremist organisation that, some years earlier, had committed a horrible slaughter of tourists in Luxor, an architectural pearl of Ancient Egypt, was appointed its governor.

Society found itself split. Secular figures undertook another revolution, which was again supported by the military. Why? It was because the Muslim Brothers launched, without limitation, property redistribution, and about one-third of Egypt's industry was owned by the military. The danger arose that the Brothers would slip their hand in the military's pocket, and the military could not afford that. The army took the side of the rebellious people and arrested the president and a number of Islamist leaders. The army and the police broke up Islamist demonstrations, several hundred people being killed. Blood is between them now, and this is serious; hence, the military is entrenching itself in power. If free elections raise Islamists to power, they will hang the generals. Fifteen years ago, the military scored a bloodless coup in Turkey, suppressing Islamists. At present, power belongs to moderate and clever Islamists who have been riding the ground swell of economic upswing, while hundreds of military men – generals and officers – have been put in prison. Egypt knows about this precedent.

The United States is at a loss; to all appearance, it does not know what to do: you go to the right and find that you have come to the left; you go to the left and find that you have come to the right; you go right ahead and find that you have come back. Americans helped to train the Egyptian military and used to cooperate with them very well. However, what about democracy and free elections? The United States suspended military aid to Egypt ($1.3 billion). However, a representative of Saudi Arabia handed over $12 billion to the military "for rescue" on behalf of the king and oil monarchies. Most likely, this will be enough for six months: $12 billion for a population of 90 million is not bad, but it is not too much as well. It is difficult to say what will follow.

Except for Qatar, all the monarchies are against the Muslim Brothers because, in a state of euphoria, the latter began to speak out against Arabian regimes as well: they had won in Egypt and were sure that they could do the same in the countries of the Persian Gulf. However, this plan failed.

Today, the military in Egypt are oriented to cooperation with Russia. We return this 'love' because internal policy in the Arab countries is not our business. Russia is not the Soviet Union, and we have neither the messianic commitment nor the economic possibilities of the Soviet past. Of course, we would really appreciate it if nongovernmental and other organizations and business circles were more active and supported the development of cooperation. However, our business is not quite fit for international activity: it seeks immediate profit, but it is not influential in serious matters.

It is useful to stress again that Arab countries are different. Why was there no such unrest in Morocco and Jordan? The main reason is that they are ruled by kings, who are believed to be direct descendants of the Prophet Muhammad; hence, they are legitimate in the eyes of their Muslims. In addition, these rulers are relatively young men educated in the West. They have showed flexibility and cleverness in carrying out certain reforms and letting moderate Islamists come to power. This balance is kept thus far.

Why have revolutions not happened in rich oil countries, except for Bahrain? Because there, too, monarchies have persisted for centuries; they are also legitimate. In addition, their wealth is so colossal that it makes it possible to plug all social gaps. Of importance in this respect is also the presence of the powerful layer of *ulema* (the estate of Muslim scholars and jurists) and the repression apparatus.

Can countries where Sharia dominates develop normally? Yes, they can, and we should understand this. What is Sharia? It means a set of rules, deemed to be 'wishes of Allah', which forbid or do not recommend some things, favour others, and prescribe still others. There is a "grey" zone, however, where Allah is neutral, and one can issue new laws in this zone without calling them laws. For example, Saudi Arabia calls them *talimat*, i.e., instructions. In other words, these states can function normally under Sharia and they have escaped mass protests, except for Bahrain. This small island state is ruled by a Sunni dynasty, which came there from the Arabian Peninsula, while the population largely consists of Shiites. Naturally, they were oppressed and rose in rebellion. Saudi Arabians brought their troops and, together with military units from the United Arab Emirates, helped the

102

king to retain power. Western propaganda and television took practically no notice of this.

The rebellion in Libya was caused by the same circumstances as in the other countries. However, M. Gaddafi would have suppressed this rebellion had it not been for external interference. This interference manifested itself in the fact that, exceeding the authority of the UN Security Council mandate, NATO actually bombed the way to power for the opposition over six months against all norms of international law. Among the rebels, there were special forces of the French and the British, which coordinated bombardments (more than 10000) and rocket attacks. The opposition "won", and Gaddafi was butchered. As a result, the country is split into three semi-independent provinces – Tripolitania, Cyrenaica, and Fezzan, dominated by several dozen armed groups united according to tribal, regional, and confessional principles. There is no state there, oil production is decreasing, and the economy and social life are in decline.

The opposition in Syria wanted to repeat the Libyan scenario. The Ba'ath regime went stale and turned into a dictatorship. However, this dictatorship was weighted and based on national traditions, ethno-confessional balance, and, of course, security agencies. There existed all the prerequisites for a revolution, but the regime turned out to be stronger. Individual military men defected to the opposition or to another country not to participate in action, but there were no defections of military units. Syria is a polyconfessional country. About 60–70% of the population are Sunnis; the Alawi (close to the Shia) minority, which is in power, constitutes 10%; 10% are Christians, and 10% are Kurds. Both Christians and Alawites know that, if Islamists come to power, they will literally slaughter them. When the Americans occupied Iraq, there were several hundred thousand Christians there; almost all of them left the country.

The Syrian regime has been withstanding the opposition for more than two and a half years. The regime is cruel, as is any war. Several months ago, US President B. Obama said that the "red line" of US policy in this respect was the use of chemical weapons by Syria: if the regime used them, the United States would begin striking against the governmental forces. Syrians created reserves of chemical weapons, as the phrase goes, just to be on the safe side, to keep balance with Israel, which has nuclear weapons. Chemical weapons were used in Syria anyhow. Who used them? We say that they were used by the opposition, but it could have happened that the opposition bought an officer from the chemical troops for big money and moved his family to a safe place. However, after the savage consequences caused by military inter-

103

ference in Libya, Americans do not want to make war for the sake of the victory of Islamists and Al-Qaeda.

Russia has little opportunity to influence the situation in the Arab world. However, Russia is still a member of the UN Security Council, and its opinion has weight. In the situation with Syria, the Russian leadership practically threw a lifebuoy to the US president: Syrians acceded to the Chemical Weapons Convention, involved respective commissions, and began the destruction of their chemical weapons stockpiles. This created a basis for cooperation between Russia and the United States and opened the possibility to find a political solution to the Syrian problem.

Right in front of our eyes, the United States accomplished its military interference in Iraq, Afghanistan, and Libya. As for Iraq, Americans have already spent at least $1.5 trillion on it; this is very hard even for a superpower such as the United States. Afghanistan has "swallowed" several hundred billion dollars. All this is already backbreaking for the United States. In addition, the United States is not very interested in Middle East oil. Its imports largely come from West Africa; moreover, it has learned how to produce gas from oil shale, and this gas is cheaper there than our natural gas; the United States has already begun to export it. How this will tell on the environment is another question, but today the country can satisfy its energy needs. America's military interference destroyed its target countries, brought them no further toward the triumph of democracy, and had a negative impact on American policy itself.

The United States stays in the Middle East, but the focus of its foreign policy is shifting to the Pacific region, where the giant China is gaining momentum.

I can say in conclusion that history more than once has witnessed periods of civilizational and identity crises that continued for centuries, such as, for example, the disintegration of the Roman Empire, the rise of the Arab caliphates, and the emergence of new civilizations. At present, events are so accelerated that the slow combustion of the past turns into an explosion. The revolutions and protest movements in the Arab countries prove this.

Nataliya Zherlitsyna

THE ORTHODOX GREEK COMMUNITY IN TUNISIA UNDER THE AUSPICES OF THE RUSSIAN EMPIRE (WITH REFERENCE TO AVPRI)[1]

The article tracks down the history of the patronage granted by the Russian Empire to the Orthodox Greek community residing in the Tunisia regency in the 18th–19th centuries. Russia traditionally kept the patronage of the Orthodox Turks high on the Eastern policy agenda. The Russian authorities decided to set up a consulate in Tunisia in 1869 partly because Russia was about to provide support to the local Greek community. In the 19th century the population in the Tunisia regency was as big as 400-1200 Greeks who were mainly traders. The Russian consul in Tunisia protected the interest of both individual Greeks facing a trial by the Bey and the Greek community as a whole. Throughout the 19th century, Russia managed to maintain warm and friendly relations between the Greek Orthodox Community, the Russian-Dutch Consulate and the government of the Bey of Tunis.

The borders of the Ottoman Empire were reminiscent of those of its Golden Age. From the 15th century onwards, the Ottoman Sultans conquered the best part of the Orthodox world. It was the time when the Greek migration started. The reasons for this were economic and demographic factors, imbalances between natural resources and human labour, as well as the dominance of foreigners. When it comes to the Ottoman Empire itself, a cultural and religious community called Orthodox *millet* took shape, with Greeks ruling the roost. The Orthodox world had its hierarchy with Moscow as a hub. The Orthodox East welcomed Russia's Doctrine of "Moscow as the Third Rome" and threw its weight behind the Russian rulers, self-proclaimed successors of the Byzantine Basileus (Emperor). The Russian Tzar was believed to be the bearer and the protector of the Universal Orthodoxy. "Some held that the mission of Russia was to find an answer to the so called the "Eastern Issue" and to set all the Orthodox peoples free"[2].

---

[1] First published in *Vostok (Oriens)*. Issue 6, 2014.

[2] Kapterev N.F. *Harakter otnoshenij Rossii k pravoslavnomu Vostoku v XVI i XVII stoletijah* [The character of the Russian attitude towards the Orthodox East XVI–XVII centuries]. Sergiyev Posad, 1914. P. 380.

The 18th century witnessed three simultaneous processes, namely the empowerment of Russia as it expanded to the borders of the Ottoman Empire, the weakening of the Ottomans as a result of the domestic crisis in the Empire, and the expansion of the Western countries which took over former Turkish lands. The weak Ottomans could no longer shield Orthodoxy from Catholic expansion, which tilted the balance from to Moscow's advantage. The patronage of the Orthodox Turks was traditionally considered a top priority of the Russian Eastern policy. A range of Russian-Turkish agreements and promises committed Russia to actions which would precondition its influence and power in the region. All Christians irrespective of their origin – whether Slavic or non-Slavic – fell under the protection of Russia. In the middle of the 19th century, the figures for the Ottoman Empire reached a peak of 12–14 million people, a fact used by St. Petersburg as a political and confessional leverage in relations with the Sultan's government.

The Russian patronage of the Greek Orthodox population took various shapes and forms starting from Russia's permission for Greeks to sail under the Russian flag and trade in the Black Sea harbours and ending with the war for the independence of Greek fellow believers from the Ottoman yoke.

Regarding the semi-independent states of the Barbary coast – based at Algiers, Tunis and Tripoli , Russia considered them to be de facto subordinate to the Ottoman Empire. From 1803 onwards, Russian Ambassadors to the Ottoman Porte (whose Embassy in Constantinople was the headquarters for all the Russian missions and Consulates across the Middle East and Maghreb countries) received regular messages from the Nyssens, a family of Dutch Consuls in Tunisia. The Nyssens made a deal with A.Y. Italinsky, Russian envoy in Constantinople, and G. Ratkel, a Dutch envoy to the Ottoman Porte (both represented the interests of the Russian subjects). In 1780, the name of the Nyssens family was mentioned in the diplomatic correspondence for the first time to stay there until the Russian revolution as the six generations of the Nyssens in a raw represented the Russian interest in Tunisia. It was only in the 1860s, when Russia started to recover from the humiliation of the Crimea war and to strengthen its co-operation with European countries, that the Russian MFA established a consulate in Tunisia. Russia decided to send its diplomatic envoy to Tunisia "for solicitation of the affairs of Greeks in Tunisia who have been under the Russian patronage since the olden times and in case Russian ships arrive" [3].

---

[3] Foreign Policy Archives of the Russian Empire Archive, Series 149, Turkish section (old), series 502–a, 1867, file 158. P. 3.

In the 17th century, the Greek community in Tunisia was estimated to be several hundred people who came from Thessaly, Macedonia, Crete, Cyprus and other islands of the Aegean Sea. Running trading companies, they were mainly engaged in commerce between Tunisia and an array of harbours. Being rather affluent, the community found itself in a privileged position in the regency.

Following the Greek national independence revolution dated 1821–1829, the Battle of Navarino Bay and the Russian victory over the Turks in the Russian-Turkish war dated 1828–1829, part of Greece became independent. From now on, according to the terms of the peace treaty, the Greek community in Tunisia could apply for the consular support of European states. The consulates of three countries, namely France, Britain, and Russia, offered Greeks their support. A Tunisian historian testifies to the fact that when Greeks were choosing between these consulates, religion was the decisive factor. Apart from the common Orthodox identity, the Russian consulate appealed to Greeks in that the Nyssens exerted their influence on the Bey of Tunis. When under the threat of legal persecution from the regency authorities and in the middle of a property dispute, community members could apply to the consulate for help.

According to French historian G. Ganiage, the total population of Greeks among Tunisian residents reached 250 people by 1834, with only Greeks under the patronage of the French and British consulates taken into account[4]. The estimate of L.F. Kostenko, Russian traveller who visited Tunisia in the 1870-s, was 140 people[5]. The book by K. Shater, contemporary Tunisia historian, says that in 1856 the number of Greeks in Tunisia was 1250 people. To put it another way, the Greek community came third in absolute numbers after Maltese and Italians[6]. Most Greeks in Tunisia were in trade or retail business.

Representing Russia's interests in Tunisia, the Nyssens were mostly assigned with a task of protecting the interests of the Orthodox Greek community. In 1837, the consular Nyssens "was happy enough to save the life of one Greek who was under the Russian patronage and who accidentally shot a

---

[4] Ganiage J. *La population européenne de Tunis au milieu du XIX siècle*. Paris, 1960. P. 37.

[5] Kostenko L.F. *Puteshestvie v Severnuju Afriku* [Travelling to Northern Africa]. Saint-Petersburg, 1876. P. 222.

[6] Chater Kh. *Dépendance et mutation précoloniales. La régence de Tunis de 1815 à 1857*. Tunis, 1984. P. 558.

Tunisian subject" [7]. It goes without saying that G. Nyssen provided consulate support to this Greek, taking advantage of the peace agreement. The second case on the protection of Orthodox Greeks fell in September 1840, when the Consulate received a message saying that some years previously a Greek woman had been enslaved by a Turk and remained captive on a small island near to Tunis All this time the Turk was trying to convert her to Islam by force. The Greek lady was begging for Russian patronage and for help to escape. Nyssen was received in audience by Ahmed Bey, and requested him to set this poor lady free. It took half a year of red-tape to grant her freedom.

The whole 19th century saw warm and friendly relations between the Greek Orthodox community, the Russian-Dutch Consulate and the Bey of Tunis, which is further substantiated by consular messages.In 1863, the Bey of Tunis Muhhamad Es-Sadok granted to the Orthodox community some land as large as 3,089 square kilometers in Buhayra so that they could build churches and extend their Orthodox cemetery[8]. This move was registered as a deal between the Bey and Eliya Manidachi. The consul informed Saint-Petersburg about this sign of gratitude, and the Emperor Alexandre II, in his turn, granted to the Bey of Tunis the White Eagle. Likewise, consular Nyssen was awarded the Order of Saint Stanislaus. This story had a sequel after the establishment of the French protectorate in 1883. Considering themselves the owners of the country, representatives of the French community tried to take away part of the granted land for their own benefit, with a powerful French Resident Paul Cambon exerting pressure on Bey Sidi-Ali. Neither the Bey, nor two diplomatic representatives from France and Russia managed toreach a compromise. So the Greeks decided to file a lawsuit in Paris and Saint-Petersburg simultaneously. To judge from the fact that in December 1833 A. Kala, representative of the Greek community and the priest at the church of Nikifor, accompanied by S. Siganaki and Kuglopolo sent a thank-you letter to the Russian Minister of Foreign Affairs N.K. Girs in Saint-Petersburg, this move was successful for the Greeks[9].

After the establishment of official consular relations between Russia and Tunisia in 1869, Consul K. Nyssen exchanged letters with the Russian envoy

---

[7] Foreign Policy Archives of the Russian Empire Archive, Series 180, Embassy in Constantinople, series 517 (I), 1839, file 1540. P. 4.

[8] Foreign Policy Archives of the Russian Empire Archive, Series 149, Turkish section (old), series 502–a, 1864, file 3844. P. 38.

[9] Foreign Policy Archives of the Russian Empire Archive, Series 151, Fond the political archive, series 482, 1883, file 1464. P. 11.

to the Ottoman Porte N.P. Ignatyev on a regular basis, with a premium being put on the affairs of the Orthodox community in Tunisia.

The Russian patronage was not just a mere formality. It was efficient and held in deep esteem. A vivid illustration is the 1879 case when the government of a newly-born Greece sent its consul to Tunisia but the Archimandrite Nikifor Papadakis addressed the Russian consul K. Nyssen on behalf of some members of the Orthodox community, asking him to maintain the Russian patronage.

On behalf of the Russian Imperial authorities, Duke Gorchakov allowed Consular Nyssen to officially grant Russian support to every Orthodox Greek who was not a Greek subject. In this regard, representatives sent a thank-you letter to Saint-Petersburg.

When Tunisia became a French protectorate, the life of the Greek and other communities was subjected to changes. The French colonial authorities encouraged naturalisation of Greeks in their pursuit of "*Frenchification*". Assimilation with the French led to a loss of collective Greek identity, turning Greeks into nothing but an integral part of the European settler community. So Second World War consolidated their bonds with France.

From the 1920s onwards, the Russian community in Tunisia (the one that came from Sebastopol with the remnants of the once mighty Russian Imperial fleet) was almost as numerous as the Greek one. What also testifies to the friendly relations between Greeks and Russians in Tunisia is the fact that Greek priests conducted a service in a Russian parish when their Russian counterparts were absent[10].

Once Tunisia gained national independence most Europeans, including Greeks and Russians, followed the example of the former colonisers and left the country. The 300-year-long Greek presence came to its end. This long and generally positive experience of the Orthodox community co-existing with the Muslim society contributed to the development of intergovernmental and inter-confessional relations between Tunisia, Greece and Russia, as well as to then burgeoning Tunisian society, widely known as tolerant and open-minded.

---

[10] Panova M. *Russkie v Tunise. Sud'ba jemigracii «pervoj volny»* [Russians in Tunisia. The fate of "first wave" emigration]. Moscow, Russian State University for the Humanities, 2008. P. 171.

ECONOMIC STUDIES

Abramova, Irina & Morozenskaya, Yevgeniya (Eds.) *Africa: Modern Strategies of Economic Development.* **Moscow: Institute for African Studies, RAS, 2016. 432 p. ISBN 978-5-91298-186-9.**
The monograph consists of four parts devoted to the problems of the evolution of concepts of development and paths for their implementation under different circumstances. Part 1 discusses the features of new strategies (innovation policy, public-private partnerships, reforms of the banking sector) and the possibilities of their realisation. Part 2 is concerned with the peculiarities of national strategies of socio-economic development in key African states. Economic strategies, including those related to shifts in traditional vs. modern attitudes to the future of African industry, energy, agriculture, water, and IT technologies, are analysed in Part 3. Part 4 is the largest: it includes ten chapters dedicated to reviewing economic policies that Africa's main foreign partners have developed toward the continent, as well as the influence of these policies on African economies and strategies for their development.
In general, the book looks at various strategy concepts and experiences and their irregular results in the context of social and economic changes in the modern world economy.
The summary was prepared by E. Morozenskaya, L. Kalinichenko.

Klishin, Vladimir & Pavlov, Vladimir. *The African Development Bank: Financial Strategies for Modernising African Economies.* **Moscow: Institute for African Studies, RAS, 2014. 246 p. ISBN 978-5-91298-148-7.**
The book explores the main priorities and directions of the long-term financial strategy of AfDB and other credit institutions of its Group that is aimed at facilitating the processes of modernisation of African economies and accelerating them in 2014–2020. It identifies the main blocks and elements of this strategy; demonstrates the growing role of AfDB in the economic development of African countries; and analyses various aspects of the possible entry and equity participation of Russia in AfDB. The book is intended for (a) specialists engaged in solving the pressing problem of intensifying Russia's foreign economic exchange with African countries, improving bilateral monetary, financial, credit and banking, and clearing and settlement

links,(b) undergraduate, graduate, and post-graduate students and teaching staff at economic universities and (c)managers of Russian companies of all forms of ownership that have already engaged or hold strategic interest in economic cooperation with Africa.

Klishin, Vladimir & Pavlov, Vladimir. *The African Development Bank: Methods and Mechanisms of Credit and Loan Operations and Investment Financing.* **Moscow: Institute for African Studies, RAS, 2014. 202 p. ISBN 978-5-91298-135-7.**

The book explores mechanisms of day-to-day operations and the main priorities of credit and loan and investment policies of the African Development Bank (AfDB) and other financial institutions of its Group – the African Development Fund (ADF) and the Nigeria Trust Fund (NTF) – in 2010–2013.It discusses the Bank's current methods for assessing the effectiveness of investment projects in African countries and issues of practical application of the universal classification of African countries based on the actual volume of their aggregate foreign currency-denominated debt in both public and private sectors. The book is intended for (a) specialists engaged in solving the pressing problem of intensifying Russia's foreign economic exchange with African countries, improving bilateral monetary, financial, credit and banking, and clearing and settlement links, including the possible entry of Russia into AfDB,(b) undergraduate, graduate, and post-graduate students and teaching staff at economic universities and (c)managers of Russian companies of all forms of ownership that engage in foreign trade and economic cooperation with Africa.

Matsenko, Irina & Matsenko, Sergey. *Banking Sector of African Countries: Problems and Perspectives of Development.* **Moscow: Institute for African Studies, RAS, 2016. 190 p. ISBN 978-5-91298-174-6.**

The monograph is devoted to the analysis of Africa's banking sector. It deals with a wide range of issues relating to various aspects of the functioning of the banking sector on the continent as a whole and in particular countries and sub-regions of Africa. Furthermore, the study presents a comparative review of the banking systems and regulations in Africa in comparison to other regions of the world. In this sense, this monograph largely closes the gap persisting in Russia's African studies due to the relatively small number of publications devoted to the analysis of the banking sector in African states in the past 20 years. The general conclusion of the study is that the region's banking sector has expanded remarkably in recent years, as well as gained a greater access to finance. This trend is affecting all African countries, with very few exceptions. Moreover, the on-going structural changes in the banking sector, in particular the emergence of mobile banking and pan-African banking groups, have a great potential to transform the existing banking systems, improve competition and efficiency, as well as access to finance and financial inclusion. The challenge is that regulation and supervision have not yet caught up with these developments, which creates bottlenecks for further expansion and may amount to a system risk.

Morozenskaya, Evgeniya (Ed.). *Africa: Paths Toward Economic Modernisation.* **Moscow: Institute for African Studies, RAS, 2014. 275 p. ISBN 978-5-91298-153-1.**

The book examines various problems of economic modernisation in African countries, including conceptual features and opportunities for practical implementation of modernisation models and changing the ratio of traditional and modern in the socio-economic development of individual countries and regions of the continent. Particular attention is paid to the great variety of modernisation methods and the ambiguity of their results in different social, political, and economic conditions. The authors analyse the influence of foreign direct investment on the process of economic modernisation of the continent, especially of its mineral and raw materials complex, and problems of the transfer and deployment of advanced technologies in Africa. The book is intended for researchers, students, and post-graduates studying the global economy, as well as for entrepreneurs and anyone interested in the economy of modern Africa.

Sapuntsov, Andrey. *Economic Priorities of Transnational Corporations of Developing Countries in Africa.* **Moscow: Institute for African Studies, RAS, 2015. 304 p. ISBN 978-5-91298-166-1.**

The monograph outlines the fundamental theories relating to the growth of transnational forms of production and exchange in the world economy, including aspects of organising a corresponding business by companies from developing countries. Based on the generalisation of economic prerequisites for the participation of residents of developing countries in the economic activities of multinational corporations of the Third World, theoretical and methodological provisions for the improvement of such entrepreneurial activities in Africa are formulated. Companies from such key developing countries as China, India, and Brazil have stepped up business in Africa; moreover, African countries themselves, including South Africa, Kenya and

Egypt, have become significant players in this market. The present study of the regularities in the conduct of multinational business in Africa by developing countries makes it possible to put the significance of the participation of Russian business in these projects on a modern footing. The book is intended for researchers in the fields of foreign entrepreneurship, developing and transitional economies, and graduate university students specialising in the world economy.

Kosukhin, Nikolay. *Political Leadership in Africa: the Past and the Present.* **Moscow: Institute for African Studies, RAS. 2015. 178 p. ISBN 978-5-91298-156-2.**

The monograph is devoted to one of the main problems of modern political science – political leadership. The author offers a typology of leadership in political power structures in African countries and pays much attention to the process of political change: transition from authoritarianism to democracy and political pluralism. At the same time, the author notes that features of authoritarianism are perpetuated in African leaders of the new generation. The work is of great interest for a wide circle of researchers, students, and post-graduates.

Ksenofontova, Natalia (Ed.). *Trade Unions in the Socio-Political Life of African Countries.***Moscow: Institute for African Studies, RAS, 2016. 195 p. ISBN 978-5-91298-176-0.**

The purpose of the book is to present a picture of the current state of trade unions and the trade union movement in different African countries. The process of globalisation, the onset of the neoliberal market ideology, consequences of world economic crises, and the key geopolitical shifts in international relations are viewed in the context of their impact on trade unions in African countries. The book depicts the struggle of trade unions against the deterioration in the social and material situation of workers in the course of structural economic reforms and for the increase of their role in the socio-political life of African countries.

Morozov, Valeriy et al. *Africa in the Context of Global Food Security.* **Moscow: Institute for African Studies, RAS, 2015. 288 p. ISBN 978-5-91298-165-4.**

The collective monograph reveals the place of Africa among the regions of the world in terms of providing the population with food and discusses the nature of threats to the food security of African countries. In this connection, it looks at critical issues of the economic and social development of African countries in the context of food security and at factors affecting their food security. Particular attention is paid to the analysis of the role of agriculture in the continent's food self-sufficiency, issues of agricultural investment, and the efficiency of the use of natural agricultural potential and labour resources. The work also discusses the contribution of individual EU and BRICS countries to improving food security in Africa. The monograph is intended for experts in modern problems of world development, as well as for a wide circle of readers.

Natufe, Igho & Khristina Turinskaya (Eds.) *Federalism in Africa: Problems and Perspectives.* **Moscow: Institute for African Studies, RAS, 2015. 220 p. ISBN 978-5-91298-162-3.**
Contributors to this volume provide analytical insights into African federalism. Chronologically, the papers in the book derive from two sources. First, there are those that were presented at the panel "Nigeria: 100 Years After Amalgamation" of the 13th International Conference for Africanists, hosted by the Institute for African Studies in Moscow on 27–30 May 2014. The other section (Part 1 of the book, in Russian) consists of papers presented at the round table "Problems and Perspectives of Federalism in Africa", held at the Institute for African Studies on 12 November 2014. The papers of the section are devoted to different aspects of federal structures in African countries other than Nigeria. Just like the "Nigerian" section, this section pays particular attention to the "national question" in Africa and how it relates to federalism.

Shubin, Gennady. *Conflictology of the Forthcoming Wars.* **2nd ed. Moscow: Centre for Strategic Studies, 2015. 108 p. ISBN 978-5-93883-265-7.**
The present Russian-English collection of articles is an improved and revised version of a brochure of the same name, published in 2007 in Moscow by Memories Publishing House. The book discusses an approximate distribution of the use of various types of weapons in forthcoming wars. An assessment is also made of the use of weapons in the current civil war in Ukraine.

INTERNATIONAL STUDIES

Abramova, Irina & Fituni, Leonid (Eds.). *Africa and Russia's National Interests.* **Moscow: Institute for African Studies, RAS, 2016. 150 p. ISBN 978-5-91298-183-8.**

The book is the first in the post-Soviet scientific literature to provide a comprehensive analysis of Russia's national interests in Africa in the context of fundamental trends and emerging threats in the world economy and politics. It demonstrates an increase in the geo-economic importance of Africa in the 21st century and the growing military-strategic interest of the world's leading powers towards the continent. The authors evaluate the prospects for economic expansion in sub-Saharan Africa and the investment potential of the region from the point of view of Russia's strategic interests, including their regional and sectoral aspects. Recommendations on practical steps to ensure Russia's national economic interests in Africa are formulated.

Bondarenko, Dmitri & Kulkova, Olga (Eds.). *International Conference "Non-Western Europe and Africa: Connections in the Past and the Present". Moscow, Russia. June 2-3, 2016: Electronic book of abstracts.* **Moscow: Institute for African Studies, RAS, 2016. 56 p. ISBN 978-5-91298-169-2.**

The book is a collection of conference abstracts of the participants of the international conference "Non-Western Europe and Africa: Connections in the Past and the Present" (Moscow, 2-3 June 2016). The abstracts are divided into four thematic sections: historical links between countries of Eastern and Central Europe and Africa; political and economic ties; cultural relations; and African students and migrants in countries of non-Western Europe. The abstracts expose a wide range of relations between countries of Central and Eastern Europe and the African continent over a long period of time.

The summary was prepared by T.L. Deich

Deich, Tatiana. *China "Conquers" Africa.* **Moscow: Institute for African Studies, RAS, 2014. 382 p. ISBN 978-5-9128-139-5.**

The book by T. Deich expands the series of the author's works dedicated to China's Africa policy. The work contains an analysis of the most important aspects of modern Chinese-African political and economic relations. The book consists of six chapters. The first two chapters provide an analysis of

China's role in the world economy and international relations in the 21st century. Chapter 3 is devoted to the political strategy of Beijing in Africa, Chapter 4 – to Beijing's economic strategy. Chapter 5 examines China's bilateral relations with a number of countries of the continent, including South Africa, Angola, Mozambique, Sudan, South Sudan, Nigeria, and Zimbabwe. Chapter 6 focuses on the interaction of China with African countries in the world arena – in the UN and BRICS, and its involvement in the settlement of conflicts and peacekeeping on the continent. The last section of the chapter deals with China's competition with Africa's traditional partners – the US and European countries, as well as with new emerging countries, including the fellow members of BRICS – India and Brazil.

Deich, Tatiana & Korendyasov, Evgeny (Eds.). *African Migration in the Context of Contemporary International Relations.* **Moscow: Institute for African Studies, RAS, 2015. 176 p. ISBN 978-5-91298-167-8.**

The collection of articles deals with the theme of African migration and its role in contemporary international relations. Africa is a continent where large masses of population are on the move; the number of African migrants is growing rapidly. The book looks at the reasons for the growing migration of Africans: deteriorating security, poverty, unemployment, and deepening demographic imbalances. In addition, the authors discuss the worsening situation with migrants in Europe and the growth of the number of illegal immigrants from North Africa and the Middle East. A number of articles are devoted to African migrants in the United States, China, and India, their way of life and relations with the locals. Another important topic reflected in the collection is the economic assistance that migrants render to their countries of origin. The increase in African migration and its contribution to the development of the continent prompted the African Union to call the African diaspora the "sixth zone of the development of Africa". The authors of the collection contributed to the study of this "zone", where there are still many blank spots.

The summary was prepared by T.L. Deich

Deich, Tatiana & Korendyasov, Evgeny (Eds.). *BRICS in the Year of the 7th Summit: Focus on Africa.* **Moscow: Institute for African Studies, RAS, 2015. 156 p. ISBN 978-5-91298-164-7.**

The book presents a collection of reports of participants of the round table "BRICS – Africa: Reconfiguration of the International Priorities of African Countries", held at the Institute for African Studies on 3 December 2014. Part 1 of the collection is devoted to general problems and prospects of

BRICS, as well as to how it is viewed by the traditional international players – the US and the EU. The part covers such topics as the results of BRICS activities over 6 years, the economic situation in member countries, the establishment of the New Development Bank of BRICS, and problems of education in the practice of BRICS. The part also touches on issues of Russia's strategy within BRICS, as well as on the role of Brazil as the bridge between BRICS and South America and Africa. Part 2 of the collection examines BRICS policy in Africa in general, its achievements and problems. Furthermore, it analyses the interaction of BRICS with Africa in the fields of military-technical cooperation, "green technologies", the development of bauxite and energy resources, food security, and conflict resolution in Africa. The part also focuses on the role of China and India as members of BRICS, as well as on the contribution of multinational corporations from BRICS countries to the economic development of Africa.

The summary was prepared by T.L. Deich

Deich, Tatiana & Korendyasov, Evgeny (Eds.). *New Partners of Africa: the Influence on the Growth and Development of the Continent.* **Moscow: Institute for African Studies, RAS, 2016. 218 p. ISBN 978-5-91298-177-7.**

The past two decades have born witness to the most significant expansion of the external economic cooperation of the African continent since the beginning of the post-colonial period. Almost all new partners, including the BRICS countries, many other emerging countries, or simply non-Western partners, belong to the non-Western world. Today, the new partners account for more than 30% of the continent's external trade turnover and the inflow of foreign investment. The present monograph examines the impact of the new partnership on the economic growth of African countries and the role and place of Africa in world politics and economy. Particular attention is paid to the relation between the aforementioned issues and the formation of a new architecture of international relations and international development assistance in the context of the emerging polycentric world.

The summary was prepared by T.L. Deich

Deich, Tatiana & Korendyasov, Evgeny & Kulkova, Olga & Zhukov, Alexander (Eds.). *Africa's Growing Role in World Politics.* **Moscow: Institute for African Studies, RAS, 2014. 298 p. ISBN 978-5-91298-147-0.**

The book is a collection of English-language articles devoted to contemporary foreign policy problems of African countries and relations between Africa and the world's leading countries. It analyses various aspects of the

118

present political and economic situation on the African continent, which reflect the growing role of African countries in contemporary international relations.

Chapter 1 presents articles on global and regional problems of Africa, primarily on issues of security and conflict resolution. It also looks at Africa's position in the modern world and contemporary international relations. Chapter 2 deals with relations between Africa and the traditional partners – the US, the EU, and Japan, as well as a relatively new player – South Korea. Chapter 3 focuses on BRICS's policy in Africa. BRICS is a new actor that has paid growing attention to African countries and successfully competed with the West for influence on the continent. Chapter 4 presents articles on Africa's largest donor and investor and BRICS's leading player – China. Chapter 5 covers Russian-African relations in the past and present. Finally, Chapter 6 highlights policies of the other BRICS member countries – India, Brazil, and South Africa, – which are also very active on the African continent.

The summary was prepared by T.L. Deich

Filippov V.R. *"Françafrique": The Shadow of the Élysée Palace over the Black Continent.* Moscow: Goryachaya liniya – Telekom, 2016. 382 p. ISBN 978-5-9912-0643-3.

The monograph deals with the complex political phenomenon of "Françafrique", practically unexplored in Russian African Studies. The book looks at it from different perspectives: as a doctrine of French neo-colonialism, a political practice of the Élysée Palace on the Black Continent, and a lobbyist network linking the political, military, and financial elites of the Fifth Republic and African elites that used to be part of the French colonial empire until the mid-20th century. The author elucidates reasons for the formation of the Françafrique system during the presidency of Charles de Gaulle and its evolution over the history of the Fifth Republic and until the present time, as well as examines the methods of the implementation of this particular doctrine of French neo-colonialism and its most notable manifestations on the Black Continent. The work is intended for diplomats, public relations officers, researchers, and graduate and post-graduate students studying international relations, public administration, public relations, political science, marketing, and management.

Lileev, Ivan. *The Old World and Africa.* Moscow: Institute for African Studies, RAS, 2015. 109 p. ISBN 978-5-91298-157-9.

The work is devoted to the current state of relations between united Europe and Africa. The focus of the book is put on the involvement of the European Union as a new actor on the international political scene in peace-making in Africa, overcoming the continent's economic backwardness, and preventing uncontrolled migration. The evolving status of united Europe, which is acquiring features of a new quasi-state entity, as well as the new positive dynamics of the development of many African countries, give the subject of the study a particular relevance.

Shubin, Gennady. *Certain Features of the Heavy Weapons Market in Africa (an Illustrated Essay).* **Moscow: Vorobyov A.V. Publisher, 2015. 128 p. ISBN 978-5-93883-251-0.**

The publication offers a comprehensive examination of the types of wea-pons and military hardware used in African wars. The book explains why only few African countries possess large-calibre heavy artillery pieces and self-propelled artillery systems of Soviet, Russian, and American origin, and why Africans prefer old Soviet howitzers and long-range cannons or their Chinese copies, and less frequently – the relatively modern British artillery pieces or obsolete American artillery pieces. The work is written on the basis of memo-ries of veterans of conflicts and participants of UN peacekeeping missions, as well as on the basis of Russian and foreign specialised publications.

Urnov, Andrey. *Africa: Policy of Barack Obama's Administration. 2009-2014.* **Moscow: Institute for African Studies, RAS, 2015. 208 p. ISBN 978-5-9128-161-6.**

The book by A. Urnov is the first in Russia to touch on Africa policy of the administration of US President Obama in 2009–2014. It analyses the "pil-lars" of the policy and the course of its implementation in the political, eco-nomic, humanitarian, and military fields. Part 1 of the book examines US policy towards Africa against the backdrop of the 2012 presidential election. Particular attention is given to the debate on Africa during the 2012 presiden-tial election campaign. Part 1 also examines the US position on conflict situa-tions on the continent, as well as bilateral relations between the United States and particular African countries. Part 2 is devoted to discussing the prepara-tion and holding of the Africa-US Leaders Summit in August 2014. It con-tains five chapters: Chapter 1 "2013: the activity of the US on the continent is increasing"; Chapter 2 "2014: the Year of Africa in the US"; Chapter 3 "More on bilateral relations (2013–2014)"; Chapter 4 "Conflict zones"; Chapter 5 "The Year of Africa is over. What's next?" The author concludes that an increase in US engagement with the continent will aggravate the competition in Africa, because China, Japan, India, the EU, and other world actors will not surrender their interests there. This may help Africa pursue a policy of balancing and playing on the contradictions of competitors.

The summary was prepared by T.L. Deich

Urnov, Andrey. *Foreign Policy of the USSR in the Years of the Cold War and "New Thinking".* Moscow: ZFK-Imidzh Lab, 2014. 683 p. ISBN 978-5-93905-063-0.

In his monograph, A. Urnov examines the main stages and the most important events of Soviet foreign policy, including its African policy since the end of the Second World War and until the collapse of the USSR. The author proceeds from the premise that the USSR consistently defended its national interests on the international arena, including the African continent, until the second half of the 1980s, despite some policy errors and miscalculations (e.g. the 1962 Cuban Missile Crisis, the deployment of Soviet troops to Afghanistan in 1979). Much attention is paid to the position of the USSR on the colonial problem and the fundamental principles and evolution of Soviet policy in the Third World, including Africa. In the monograph, two chapters of Part 1 "The Cold War" deal with Soviet policy in North Africa, the Horn of Africa, Sub-Saharan Africa, and the liberation struggle in the Portuguese colonies and in Southern Africa. Part 2 "New Thinking" examines the role of the USSR in the final stages of the "second independence war" of Angola and the decolonisation of Namibia, as well as in the events that paved the way for the dismantling of the apartheid regime in South Africa.

The summary was prepared by T.L. Deich.

Zherlitsyna, Natalia. *Russian-Tunisian relations. 1780–1991.* Moscow: Institute for African Studies, RAS, 2014. 219 p. ISBN 978-5-91298-144-9.

The monograph considers the history of Russian-Tunisian relations on a wide temporal scale, which allows the author to draw a comprehensive picture of their formation and development and assess the dynamics and main directions of interaction at various historical stages. An extensive study of the history of the development of relations between the two countries enables the readership to trace the origin and development of trends that determine the current state of bilateral relations. The research is based on materials from archives, Soviet newspapers and journals, and memoirs.

SOCIO-CULTURAL STUDIES

Babaev, Kirill & Arkhangelskaya, Alexandra. *What is Africa?* **Moscow: Ripol classic, 2015. 480 p. ISBN 978-5-386-08595-7.**
The book is a popular scientific description of the most fascinating aspects of African Studies: its nature and fauna, peoples and languages, religions and cultures, art and architecture. The authors – well-known Africanists – use a simple and accessible language to speak about the most intriguing mysteries of the Black Continent, amazing customs of African peoples, and little-known pages of their history. The book presents original materials and has no analogues in modern Russian literature in terms of its style and scope. It will undoubtedly play an important role in popularising long-accumulated diverse knowledge about the African continent and its inhabitants, and will thus re-awaken a scientific interest in Africa that has now largely faded. The book is intended for a wide circle of people who are interested in studying the surrounding world, as well as for university and high school students.

Banshchikova, Anastasia. *Female Images in the Works of Art of Ancient Egypt.* **Moscow: Lenand, 2014. 168 p. ISBN: 978-5-397-04577-3.**
This book explores the evolution of female images in ancient Egyptian literature over practically all periods of its development, beginning with texts of the Old Kingdom and finishing with late demotic works. On materials of three different genres – ancient Egyptian tales and novels, didactic works, and love lyrics – the author considers the functioning and development of female characters and analyses their structure, features, artistic means, the role of plots, and interplay with male characters. A literary analysis is applied to draw conclusions about the place and role of women in ancient Egyptian society as a whole: there is a tendency to gradual deterioration of the attitude towards the woman – from a fairly harmonious vision of her as a beloved wife in texts of the Old Kingdom to disregard of women in texts of the Late Period, which depict them as absolutely spoiled and unworthy creatures. The book is designed for a wide circle of readers interested in culture, literature, and social life of ancient Egypt.

Banshchikova, Anastasia. *Turning Points in the Historical Tradition and Consciousness of the Ancient Egyptians According to Sources from the Late 2ⁿᵈ Millennium BCE – 1ˢᵗ Millennium CE.* **Moscow: Lenand, 2015. 208 p. ISBN 978-5-9710-1511-6.**

The book explores how turning points of the history of ancient Egypt associated with foreign invasions (the Hyksos invasion, the Sea People's raids, the invasions by Nebuchadnezzar II and Cambyses) are reflected in ancient Egyptian historical and literary tradition, up to the Coptic stage of its development and the latest Arab-Muslim views. The author reveals the centuries-old evolution of the examined subjects: their historic core, the nature and mechanisms of fictionalisation, folklorisation, refraction and selection of historical facts and memories. The monograph analyses a number of the phenomena of the historical consciousness and memory of the ancient Egyptians and characteristics and models of perception of their country's past. The book is intended for a wide circle of readers interested in culture, literature, and history of ancient Egypt.

Baskin, Ken & Bondarenko, Dmitri. *The Axial Ages of World History: Lessons for the 21st Century.* **Litchfield Park: ISCE PUB, 2014. 152 p. ISBN 978-1-938158-14-8.**
Our world today has become so globalised, so socially and technologically complex that current ideas and institutions haven't enabled us to address our most pressing problems. From global warming to possible food, water, and energy shortages, these challenges demand international cooperation; yet, that cooperation has proven impossible among today's nations. This is not the first time in world history that existing societies could not address the challenges of rapid change. In *The Axial Ages of World History*, Ken Baskin and Dmitri M. Bondarenko compare the modern world's dilemma with that of a similar period, the Axial Age (800-200 BCE). In both the Axial Age and Modernity (1500 CE–present), forces of increasing social and technological complexity drove the societies moving through them to transform the way people in them thought about the world and governed themselves. The book explores how this transformation, from the chaos of failed institutions to the order of newly evolved ways of living together, occurred in axial Greece and China and in modern Western Europe – in waves of horrific wars, experiments in new types of government, and in radical spiritual renewals. While the authors emphasise that there is no way to predict which of many possible outcomes will occur, in the book's conclusion, they share some thoughts on actions people can begin taking today to improve that outcome, whatever it might be.

Bondarenko, Dmitri. *The Shades of Black: Cultural-Anthropological Aspects of Mutual Perceptions and Relations Between African Americans* *and African Migrants in the U.S.A.* **Moscow: YASK Publishing House, 2016. 232 p. ISBN 978-5-94457-248-7.**

In the 17th–19th centuries, Black communities of the descendants of people who had been forcibly removed from Africa by slave traders formed in the New World. In the United States of America they presently constitute 12.6% of the population – 39.9 from 316.1 million people. Voluntary migration from Africa to the USA began at the same time that slavery was abolished – in the 1860s, but its scale remained small until the 1980s–1990s. In the late 1990s, migration from Africa to the USA intensified dramatically, and by 2013 the number of sub-Saharan Africa natives in the country reached 1.4 million. Despite common roots, there is a considerable social distance between African Americans and Africans. This contradicts the postulates of a number of powerful intellectual, cultural, and political trends that began to spread since the mid-19th century. Garveyism, Pan-Africanism, Afrocentrism, and other teachings of this kind insist on the single spiritual and mental background of all Black people wherever they were born, the worldwide "black brotherhood" and the presence of goals and tasks that are common for all the people of "black race", and demand their concerted actions in the world ruled by the Whites. However, until recently, the relations between the Black communities of the two hemispheres were largely virtual. When a real "meeting" took place with the current wave of migration of Africans to the USA, it became clear that many important differences of all sorts had formed between them over the centuries of separate existence.

As our respondent said, "it's still very hard for Africans to accept African Americans. Also for African Americans to accept Africans: a lot of African Americans see Africans as just any other foreigners". Among the reasons for this, the peculiarity of mutual perceptions plays a significant part. To a considerable degree, this peculiarity is determined by social factors, but cultural are no less important. Some aspects of the mutual perceptions of Africans and African Americans are connected with different refraction in the both groups' collective memory and mass consciousness of important events of the past. The other aspects are related to today's experience of intercultural interaction. Our fieldwork was done in seven states (Alabama, Illinois, Massachusetts, Minnesota, Missouri, New York, and Pennsylvania), in towns and medium-size cities such as St. Louis MO, Boston, Chicago, Minneapolis, New York City, and Philadelphia, in 2013–2015. In total, 196 structured interviews and non-structured conversations were recorded and observations of many public and private events in the lives of African Americans and African migrants were documented.

Bondarenko, Dmitri (Ed.). *Collection of Works of theYoung Scholars' Council of the Institute for African Studies of the RAS.* **Vol. 1. Moscow: Institute for African Studies, RAS, 2014. 265 p. ISBN 978-5-91298-158-6.**
The collection publicises the research conducted by young Africanists in different disciplines in 2009-2014. The books presents works of employees and post-graduates of the Institute for African Studies and the Peoples' Friendship University of Russia, who are actively engaged in research in the field of African Studies. The problems covered by the authors are broad and reflect the complexity of analysing modern Africa. The authors consider their topics through different lenses – from culturology and history to international law.

Bondarenko, Dmitri & Demintseva, Ekaterina (Eds.). *Africa: Processes of Socio-Cultural Transformation.* **Moscow: Institute for African Studies, RAS, 2014. 177 p. ISBN 978-5-91298-125-8.**
Over the past decade Africa has been involved in the turbulent processes of transformation and globalisation. However, the traditional way of life does not disappear in African countries, but adapts to modern conditions. The contributors to the volume demonstrate, with different examples, social, cultural, and religious features of the development of African countries.

Sledzevsky, Igor (Ed.). *Africa's Civilizational Alternatives.* **Volume I. Part 1. Moscow: Institute for African Studies, RAS, 2016. 212 p. ISBN 978-5-91298-180-7;**
Africa's Civilizational alternatives. **Volume I. Part 2. Moscow: Institute for African Studies, RAS, 2016. 158 p. ISBN 978-5-91298-185-2.**
What are the main directions of the modern civilizational development of Sub-Saharan Africa? What role does the cultural self-determination of the peoples of Africa play in choosing the basic framework for such development – its ideals, values, principles of social organisation – under the conditions of the crisis of the post-colonial model of dependent development and the escalation of destructive processes in the region since the end of the 20th century? These are some of the questions posed by the authors of this collective monograph. The monograph was conceived as part of a multi-volume publishing project "Civilizational Alternatives of Africa" of the Centre for Civilizational and Regional Studies of the Institute for African Studies. Volume 1 is devoted to the civilizational potentialities and civilizational vectors of modern African development. The authors chose the fundamental problem of the civilizational vectors of world develop-

ment, world politics, and international relations in the conditions of global-isation as the starting point of the volume. The main subject of the study is religious experience and spiritual renewal of modern African societies amidst the rise of religious consciousness in the world and the division of the geocivilizational space of the continent between Islam and Christianity. The results of the research can be used in the field of political forecasting and in monitoring risks and threats of increasing social and political insta-bility in countries of Sub-Saharan Africa.

Sosnovsky, Nikolai. *Rastafarian Culture.* **Moscow: Institute for Afri-can Studies, RAS, 2016. 300 p. ISBN 978-5-91298-172-2.**

The book by the famous Russian Africanist, culturologist, and publicist N. Sosnovsky is devoted to the phenomenon of the informal youth subculture Rastafari (rasta-reggae, rasta, the Rastafari movement), little studied in Rus-sian science, but significant and widely known in the youth environment. Combining an objective scientific analysis with an "immersion" in the in-sights of styles, values, and meanings of the youth subculture, which is close to the author, N. Sosnovsky speaks about the place and role of Rastafarianism in raising the cultural awareness of the African diaspora and African peoples and their opposition to the cultural hegemony of the West. Based on exten-sive and original materials, the book describes the fascinating history of the emergence and development of rasta as a musical style and a subculture that originated in Jamaica and then gained wide popularity among the African diaspora of the West Indies and Europe and the urban youth in African coun-tries. The monograph details the evolution of the Rastafari movement – from a syncretic and original African-Christian cult to a mass version of Pan-African ideology, and then to a subculture – a youth cultural style that re-flects the attitudes and values of African cultural nationalism. The author meticulously and convincingly reveals the role of the Rastafari movement of the African diaspora in the modernisation of the culture of the African city, the popularisation of the image of Africa in the countries of the West, and the evolution of African cultural nationalism. The reader will also find here a detailed analysis of sources and literature on the subject of Rastafari. The work is intended for specialists and a wide circle of readers interested in in-formal youth subcultures, African-Christian cults and movements, and the philosophy of African nationalism.

Tatarovskaya, Irina. *Myths of the Peoples of Tropical and Southern Africa: the Foundation of the Spiritual and Social Life of African Society.*

Moscow: Institute for African Studies, RAS, 2016. 194 p. ISBN 978-5-91298-171-5.
The book presents and examines myths that had never been translated before (with a few exceptions) and had not been investigated in terms of their structure and rational meaning. The myths are grouped into eight chapters according to their themes. Particular attention is paid to cosmogonic myths, the pantheon of deities in African mythology, the essence and origins of life and death, anthropogenesis, the essence and origins of totems. African mythology is symbolic, zoototemic, and zoocosmic. The author reveals the meaning of such concepts as heavenly bodies and classical elements (fire, air, water, earth). Many of the myths presented in the book are devoted to the problem of the "spirits" of individual objects and living beings. Some myths expose the social structure of African society. Myths of the peoples of Tropical and Southern Africa provide an opportunity to understand the rational meaning of African mythology and view them as the gold fund of African civilization.

GENDER STUDIES

Ilyina, Nadezhda & Ksenofontova, Natalia. *Man and Woman. Portraits. Masks. Characters. Volume 5.* Moscow: Institute for African Studies, RAS, 2014. 197 p. ISBN 978-5-912981-51-7.

Identity issues, from whichever perspective they are considered, invariably arouse interest not only among professional researchers, but also among ordinary people. When they concern men and women, their mutual perceptions and their characters, it is all the more so... Despite the fact that this publication is scientific, it is quite likely that the reader who has accidentally taken up this book will not set it aside. Gender Studies are not a new phenomenon in Russia, but only over the past decade they have become particularly noticeable, and – it should be noted – not without the efforts of the Group for Gender Studies of the Institute for African Studies. This book is another – and very successful – attempt to expand the boundaries of perceiving the feminine and masculine and find unity and harmony in the two seemingly very different world orders. The monograph is devoted to female writers: novelists, memoirists, and diarists from Africa, Russia, and Europe. Part 1 focuses on Nigerian writers, which unfortunately are little known to the Russian reader (N. Ilyina writes about Igbo writers Flora Nwapa, Ifeoma Okoye, Buchi Emecheta, Chimamanda Ngozi Adichie). Part 2 discusses women's identity, the "mirrors" that reflect it, and the masks that women – not the weaker sex after all, as this book shows – put on.

Krylova, Natalia & Ksenofontova, Natalia (Eds.). *Public, Political, and Cultural life of African Countries in the Gender Dimension.* Moscow: Institute for African Studies, RAS, 2014. 406 p. ISBN 978-5-91298-150-0.

The book is a multifaceted study of the social, political, and cultural life of African countries as viewed through the prism of gender relations. The authors include experts from Russia, France, the United States, and African countries (Zambia, Nigeria, Cote d'Ivoire). Special attention is paid to power relations, interaction of tradition and innovation, changes in the sphere of value systems, stereotypes of behaviour and thinking, ethic and aesthetic views, and rethinking identities. A number of chapters feature portraits of political and public leaders, prominent figures of literature and art.

Krylova, Natalia & Ksenofontova, Natalia (Eds.). *Violence and Terrorism. The Gender Aspect.* **Moscow: Institute for African Studies, RAS, 2016. 278 p. ISBN 978-5-91298-170-8.**

The 20th century – the age of ambiguous global transformations on the planet – has aggravated the situation in African and Eastern societies, many of which are undergoing serious social transformations engendered by various kinds of conflicts – political, economic, ethno-religious, and socio-cultural. The centuries-old systems of relations between people, families, communities, ethnicities, states, and regions are being destroyed and reconstructed. What is the role of women in the complex systems of different oppositional states and relations? How strong and what is the reason for their desire to overcome these processes? The present collective monograph aims at answering these questions.

Ksenofontova, Natalia. *We Are the Two Arms of the Same Cross. TheAnthropology of Gender. Essays.* **Moscow: Institute for African Studies, RAS, 2015. 644 p. ISBN 978-5-91298-154-8.**

Reconstructing the features and dynamics of gender relations in various socio-cultural environments, the author turns to a wide factual material – from the traditional societies of Africa, the East, Latin America, and the ancient societies of Greece and Rome to the modern societies of Russia, Europe, and the New World. The book focuses on revealing the causes of gender inequality and the formation of stereotypes of mass gender consciousness. The author pays special attention to the search for those ways and to the methods that a woman chooses for the assertion of her self-sufficient personality, the representation of corporality, and the emancipation of feelings. The book looks at the origins of the appearance of such a 20th century phenomenon as a "new woman", which managed to unfold her unique individuality and creative potential in the fields of art, literature, and philosophy. A significant place is given to the history of women's clothing, which manifests itself as a mirror or a mask of identity.

NORTH AFRICAN STUDIES

Isaev, Leonid & Savateev, Anatoly (Eds.); Vasiliev, Alexey (general editorship). *The Arab Crisis and its International Implications.* **Moscow: Lenand, 2014. 256 p. ISBN 978-5-9710-1260-3.**

The monograph offers the reader a comprehensive analysis of the socio-political upheaval in a number of major Arab states that were to a certain degree affected by the events of the Arab Spring. The authors of the book attempt to analyse the events that took place in 2011–2013 over the entire Arabic-speaking belt from Morocco to Iraq with a view to forming the reader's understanding of the phenomenon of the so-called Arab Spring to the fullest possible extent. In the framework of this work, the authors look at the prerequisites of the popular unrest, the main actors and driving forces, describe the course of events, and outline the main internal and international consequences, which are becoming increasingly acute and drag European, Asian, and Tropical African states into the maelstrom. The authors intend the monograph for specialists and a wide circle of readers interested in modern trends and risks of socio-political development in general and in MENA countries in particular. The research draws on the results of the project "Monitoring risks of socio-political destabilisation", which was carried out within the framework of the 2013 Fundamental Research Programme of the Higher School of Economics.

Isaev, Leonid & Shishkina, Alisa. *The Arab World in the Digital Epoch: Social Media as a Form of Political Activity.* **Moscow: Lenand, 2014, 128 p. ISBN 978-5-9710-1030-2.**

The book centres on the impact of information technology in the Arab world in the period 2011-2012. It describes the latest information technology tools and mechanisms and consequences of censorship and the interplay between informatization and socio-political processes in a society.

Kisriev, Enver & Savateev, Anatoly (Eds.). *Islamic Radical Movements on the Political Map of the Modern World: Countries of North and North-East Africa.* **Moscow: URSS, 2015. 424 p. ISBN 978-5-9710-2138-4.**

What is behind the notion of "Islamic radicalism"? Why, how, and where did it originate? What historical and social role does it perform in the Muslim Ummah and the world as a whole? These are some of the questions the authors of the collective multi-volume monograph are trying to answer. The first volume is devoted to one of the main regions where radical movements are particularly noticeable – to North and North-East Africa. It explores the geography of the spread of Islam, ideological and philosophical foundations of Islamic radical movements, and their relations with the state, society, and the outside world. The authors believe that radical forces use Islamic doctrines as an excuse for extremism. At the same time, they believe that radicalism and political Islam are provoked by the West, its contempt for the values of Islamic civilization, and the desire to use extremist forces against unwanted regimes. It is proven that the aggravation of radical tendencies in Islam is a recurring phenomenon. The publication, which is designed to cover the largest possible number of countries with Muslim population, has no analogues in domestic and world Islamic studies. The research is intended for scientists, teachers, and students, as well as for anyone who is interested in the latest trends in the evolution of the Islamic world and geopolitical changes.

Kostelyanets, Sergey. *Darfur: A History of the Conflict.* **Moscow: Institute for African Studies, RAS, 2014. 388 p. ISBN 978-5-91298-146-3.**
The conflict in the Darfur region of Sudan is considered one of the greatest humanitarian disasters of the 21st century. The monograph examines the causes and historical background of the Darfur conflict and domestic, regional, and international factors that have determined its dynamics, as well as analyses the attempts to resolve it. The author explores such destructive phenomena that predetermined the escalation of violence in the region as the socio-economic marginalisation of peripheral areas of the country, the removal of regional leaders from the decision-making process at the national level, and the provision of the government's support to some tribal militias against others. The book studies the process of transformation of local disputes over access to natural resources and of clashes between individual armed groups, as well as between the rebels and the regular army units, into a "war of all against all". A special attention is paid to the analysis of the activities of the peacekeeping missions of the UN and the African Union in Darfur.

Savateev, Anatoly & Sledzevsky, Igor. *Protest Movements in Arab Countries: Drivers, Features, Perspectives. Materials of the Round Table.* **2nd ed. Moscow: URSS, 2015. 124 p. ISBN 978-5-9710-2004-2.**
The collection contains the most interesting and relevant presentations of the participants of the conference dedicated to the 2011 events in the Arab world, held at the Institute for African Studies. In a broad context, the authors

discuss the nature of popular uprisings ("political upheaval", "sedition", a revolution of regional or even global significance, a prologue of such a revolution?), the likelihood of a "social media revolution" spreading to neighbouring countries of Tropical Africa, the prospects for a democratic process in the Muslim World, and positions and perspectives of the "new Islam". In this context, the experience of modern political development of Iran and Turkey and the regional and civilizational features of the political process in North and Tropical Africa are considered and analysed. Much attention is paid to the dynamics of the socio-demographic development of the region as one of the main factors for the growth of political instability.

Shubin, Gennady. *Heavy Weapons of Future Civil Wars in Arab Countries (a Short Essay).* **Moscow: Vorobyov A.V. Publisher, 2015. 92 p. ISBN 978-5-93883-279-4.**

The monograph attempts to predict the main types of weapons that can be used in potential future war in Arab countries. It offers a detailed analysis of heavy weaponry. Interestingly, it draws a curious conclusion that in the event of an armed conflict, Arabs may even use small arms dating back to the late 19th century, which are still kept in families and are fit for use. The book is in two languages – Russian and English.

Tkachenko, Alexander (Ed.) *The Middle East and North Africa: the Problem of Modernization and International Security.* **Moscow: Institute for African Studies, RAS, 2016. 376 p. ISBN 978-5-91298-175-3.**

The book explores the processes of modernisation in the countries of the region of the Middle East and North Africa (MENA) that primarily took place in the 2000s. It analyses the key political, economic, and social elements of modernisation and the impact they have had on the development of MENA states, as well as how they relate to the problems of international security and local, regional, and global conflicts.

The first chapter discusses the origins and root causes that gave rise to the phenomenon of modernisation in MENA countries at the turn of the second and third millennia in the context of globalisation and the system crisis of traditional authoritarian political structures. The second chapter examines the progress of reforms. Considerable attention is paid to the study of the Arab Spring, more precisely – of the causes and origins of the unprecedented political upheaval that swept the countries of the region in the late 2000s – early 2010s. The third chapter presents a picture of the Arab East in the light and dynamics of the changing world order. The fourth chapter discusses the role of external factors in the Middle East conflict, opportunities, and obstacles on the way towards its settlement, and the impact on international security. The fifth chapter concludes the study with an analysis of the two opposite mega-trends in political, economic, and social transformation of the region – the centrifugal and the centripetal ones. The publication is intended for a wide circle of readers – researchers and international practitioners, teachers and students.

Tokarev, Andrey et al. *Memories of Veterans of Military-Political Assistance to Algeria.* **Moscow: Institute for African Studies, RAS, 2014. 168 p. ISBN 978-5-91298-132-6; ISBN 978-5-7777-0584-6.**
The collection of memories is dedicated to the history of Soviet and Russian military-political assistance to Algeria over half a century (from the early 1960s to the present). The handbook offers unique facts recounted by authors of the memories. The book includes original photo documents from authors' personal archives. The memories complement the previously published memories of veterans of military conflicts in other African countries, enriching the picture of military-political cooperation of the USSR and Russia with countries of the continent.

Vasiliev, Alexey et al. *Cooperation Between the Russian Federation and the Arab Republic of Egypt: Opportunities and Constraints.* **I.S. Ivanov (Ed.) Russian International Affairs Council (RIAC). Moscow: Spetskniga, 2015. 22 p. ISBN 978-5-91891-439-7.**
The Russian Federation and the Arab Republic of Egypt are tied by an intricate web of historical linkages in politics, economics, and cultural affairs. Cooperation with Egypt concurs with Russia's interests in the Middle East – a region that borders Russia to the south and is one of the most geopolitically important and conflict-prone areas in the world. Accordingly, cooperation between the two countries will contribute to Russia's stable position in the Islamic world. Furthermore, it may contribute to building favourable conditions for the development of Russian regions that have a significant Muslim population. It may also help preserve and consolidate Russia's interests on the global oil and gas market, as well as on the strategically significant market for Russia's agricultural and hi-tech products, facilitate the export of goods and services within the framework of bilateral military-technical and aerospace cooperation agreements, etc. There are extensive and significant cultural ties between Russia and Egypt: considerable international tourism, the large Russian community in Egypt, and the interfaith communication

between Christians and Muslims. The goals and objectives of Russian policy in the region can better be achieved through the coordination of Russia's and Egypt's international activities on the basis of consistent consultations between the ministries of foreign affairs on matters pertaining to the United Nations, the Organisation of Islamic Cooperation, the League of Arab States, the African Union, the Gas Exporting Countries Forum,and other leading international organisations and forums.

TROPICAL AFRICAN STUDIES

Denisova, Tatyana. *Tropical Africa: the Evolution of Political Leadership.* **Moscow: Institute for African Studies, RAS, 2016. 596 p. ISBN 978-5-91298-181-4.**

Throughout the history of mankind, political leadership has played a large role in the development of individual countries and regions. Chiefs, monarchs, and politicians have for centuries been making huge contributions to the formation of societies. In recent years, growing attention has been paid to the phenomenon of political leadership, largely due to the important role it plays in modern social and political life. The book examines the processes of formation of institutions of political leadership in Tropical Africa – the region that is suffering from mismanagement more than any other. The work also provides an overview of the most common types of political leadership in the region, i.e. authoritarianism, pseudo-democracy, dictatorship, etc., in the context of African political realities. The evolution of the phenomenon of political leadership is traced from the inception of the group of founding fathers of modern independent states, who established authoritarian regimes in Tropical Africa in the late 1950s and in the 1960s, and until the advent of "democratic" leaders, who have come to replace them.

Elez, Andrei (Ed.) *ECOWAS: Problems of Regional Integration.* **Moscow: Institute for African Studies, RAS, 2016. 282 p. ISBN 978-5-91298-182-1.**

The articles included in the collective work are partly based on the materials of the round table dedicated to the 40th anniversary of ECOWAS, which was organised by the Centre for Tropical African Studies of the Institute for African Studies in 2015. These articles mostly discuss contemporary economic and political problems of the community. The articles in the book are grouped according to their either economic or political focus, although this is not reflected in the work's formal structure. A number of articles deal with problems common to ECOWAS (to the community in general or to the majority of its member states), in fact not only to ECOWAS, while other articles scrutinise specific countries in terms of their economic or political structure.

Shlenskaya, Svetlana. *The United Republic of Tanzania.* Moscow: Institute for African Studies, RAS, 2014. 261 p. ISBN 978-5-91298-136-4.

Vinogradova, Natalia & Sagoyan, Larisa. *The Central African Republic.*Moscow: Institute for African Studies, RAS, 2014. 185 p. ISBN 978-5-91298-149-4.

Vinokurov, Yuri (Ed.). *The Democratic Republic of the Congo.* Moscow: Institute for African Studies, RAS, 2014. 408 p. ISBN 978-5-91298-143-2.

In 2014, the Centre for Tropical African Studies published three reference works focusing on countries of the region. The reference book *The Democratic Republic of the Congo* was published in its first edition. The two other books were published in their second editions. The new editions reflect all political, socio-economic, and other changes in the focus countries that had taken place since the first edition. All reference works have the same structure, which is traditional for such publications. They include chapters on various aspects of the life of the country: physical and geographical characteristics, population, history, political system, economy, culture, education, health, etc. The authors relied in their research on statistics published in various foreign journals and on national statistics of the referenced countries. They collected a wealth of factual material that allowed them to draw a coherent picture of the internal situation in each country and its place in the modern world order and highlight the peculiarities of every referenced country, which are particularly easily observed by the reader due to the similar structure of the books. As a result, it is easy to compare the states represented in the reference books by various parameters. All the above-mentioned reference books include tables, maps, a list of abbreviations, a timeline of major events, as well as indexes of personal, geographical, and ethnic names, and are illustrated with colour photographs. These books are, in fact, encyclopaedic editions, which can serve as handbooks for those who are interested in a particular African country, including African Studies students, specialists in international relations, businessmen already working or planning to work with these countries, and tourists.

The summary was prepared by S.M. Shlenskaya.

Sidorova, Galina. *Africa: War of Thoughts and War of People in the Mirror of the Democratic Republic of the Congo.* Moscow: Nauka – Vostochnaja Literatura, 2015. 527 p. ISBN 978-5-02-036604-6.

The monograph analyses armed conflicts in Africa through the example of the Democratic Republic of the Congo (DRC), which remains one of the

136

most notorious 'trouble spots' in the world. The historical framework of the present work covers the period of 2011–2014. The monograph concentrates on numerous crises that have arisen due to the local specifics in the east of the DRC and in the Great Lakes region. The study is focused on the fight of the government against illegal armed groups of both Congolese and foreign origin amidst escalating violence, humanitarian shocks, impoverishment of the population, and soaring crime. The work also reviews the role of regional and international partners of the DRC that assist the country's effort to pacify the centres of tension. The emphasis is made on the political, diplomatic, and military methods of conflict resolution and crisis management, particularly on the priority of the intervention strategy of the UN Stabilisation Mission in the DRC, which has been strengthened and reconfigured with the renewal of its mandate. However, the author stresses that above all the Congolese themselves should address these threats, albeit with adequate assistance from the international community.

Fituni, Leonid (Ed.). *Southern Africa at the Present Stage.* **Moscow: Institute for African Studies, RAS, 2016. 214 p. ISBN 978-5-91298-173-9.**

The collection presents a wide range of opinions of experts – economists, historians, political scientists and anthropologists of the Institute for African Studies and other scientific and educational institutions – on the problems of development of the countries of Southern Africa, with the focus on the most industrially developed country of the continent – South Africa.

The authors note some positive developments in the post-apartheid era in South Africa and post-colonial era in Southern Africa. At the same time, however, they highlight a number of negative processes leading to growing social tensions, such as the spread of corruption and xenophobia, a slowdown in economic growth and scientific and technological progress, rising unemployment, and inequality. The situation in the region, according to the authors of the collection, reflects changes in the global balance of power: the weakening of the dominant role of the United States and the EU, the growing role of China, and the emergence of new geopolitical blocs, especially BRICS, which open new opportunities for Russian-African cooperation.

Fituni, Leonid & Shubin, Vladimir (Eds.) *South African Republic.* **Moscow: Institute for African Studies, RAS, 2014. 256 p. ISBN 978-5-91298-145-6.**

The handbook is an encyclopaedic publication about South Africa. It contains data on nature, population, history, political system, economic potential, culture, etc. of this large African state. The handbook is intended both for specialists and for a wide circle of readers.

Shubin, Gennady et al. *The Forgotten Civil War in Angola. Memories of Eyewitnesses.* **(2nd ed., in 2 vols.). Moscow: Memories, 2015. 316 p. ISBN 978-5-904935-56-6 (Vol. 1); ISBN 978-5-904935-57-3 (Vol. 2).**

This second edition, published in two volumes, continues the series of books on the civil war in Angola and Soviet military involvement in this conflict. It presents texts and memories of veterans that were not included in the first edition. Most of the memories are recorded by the book's authors and editors through interviews, so occasionally they provide a subjective assessment of the events. The work includes many original photographs from authors' personal archives.

Shubin, Vladimir. *Fates of Zimbabwe.* Moscow: Institute for African Studies, RAS, 2015. 158 p. ISBN 978-5-91298-160-9.
The book is devoted to the history of Zimbabwe from the 1960s to the present time. It examines the emergence and growth of the national liberation movement in this country, successes and problems of its post-independence development, causes and consequences of the economic and political crisis in the early 21st century, and the measures taken to overcome it. Particular attention is paid to the relations of Zimbabwe with the USSR/Russia. The book is based on materials from Russian and foreign archives, memories of participants in the events, and the author's personal experience.
The summary was prepared by T.L. Deich

Tokarev, Andrey et al. *Memories of Veterans of Military-Political Assistance to the People's Republic of Angola.* Moscow: Institute for African Studies, RAS, 2016. 180 p. ISBN 978-5-91298-188-3.
The collection of memories is dedicated to the history of Soviet military-political and military-technical assistance to the People's Republic of Angola at one of the most dramatic moments in its history: during its first year as an independent state, a civil war, and a foreign military intervention. The handbook presents unique facts recounted by the authors of the memories – the first Soviet specialists in Angola. For the first time, photo documents from authors' personal archives are published. The memories complement the previously published memories of veterans of military conflicts in other African countries, enriching the picture of military-political cooperation of the USSR and Russia with countries of the continent. The collection holds historical value and may be used as a main source.

Scientific edition

AFRICAN STUDIES IN RUSSIA

**Works of the Institute for African Studies
of the Russian Academy of Sciences**

Yearbook 2014–2016

*Утверждено к печати
Институтом Африки РАН*

Зав. РИО ИАфр РАН Н.А. Ксенофонтова

Компьютерная верстка Г.М. Абишевой

Подписано к печати 22.09.17. Объем 9 п.л.
Тираж 500 экз. Заказ № 144.

Отпечатано в ПМЛ Института Африки РАН
123001, Москва, ул. Спиридоновка, 30/1